THE
IDEA
OF
OFFICE

THE
IDEA
OF
OFFICE

K.Sietsma

Translated by Henry Vander Goot

PAIDEIA PRESS
Jordan Station, Ontario, Canada

Canadian Cataloguing in Publication Data

Sietsma, K.
    The idea of office

Translation of: Ambtsgedachte.
ISBN 0-88815-065-2

1. Clergy – Office.   2. Lay ministry.
I. Title.

BV660.2.S5313 1985   253   C84-099692-6

Translated by Henry Vander Goot.
Cover design by Gerrit V.L. Verstraete, Christian Communications Centre, Toronto.

ISBN 0-88815-065-2
Printed in Canada.

Contents

Office as Authority:
The Impact of a Biblical Idea

Though it was written many decades ago, Rev. K. Sietsma's simple essay on the idea of office is still timely today. It first appeared as a series of articles written for a popular paper and thus for general public consumption in the Reformed Christian community of pre-World War II Holland. In that context the idea of office was closely associated with the traditional Calvinistic vision, with the ideas of divine fore-ordination and the eternal decree, with the idea of the sovereignty of God and the delegated, relative sovereignty of man in the various areas of life, with the ideas of the will of God as ordering the life of man and of salvation as the life of obedient doing that comes from hearing the Word, with Christ as Lord of creation and Head of the restored covenant between God and man. The idea of office is a natural and indispensable link in this great chain of biblical truth.

We cannot restate that great vision today without referring to the idea of office. Yet we have to work hard to hear the word and recollect the idea. Modern language and ideas have drifted into our consciousness, diminishing our distinctive Reformed awareness. We reread the Bible accordingly. In an intensely anti-authoritarian, democratizing, and personalistic climate, rather than speak of office and calling, we speak of "personal relationships," "service," "sharing with others," and "using one another's gifts and talents in the church." With this language we are drifting into a new tradition, the assumptions and consequences of which we have not yet begun to realize fully.

As Rev. Sietsma shows, a similar trend appears in other areas of life. For example, in our national life the idea of office has been repressed by the cult of the person, the public hero. Stressing the need for strong and able leaders, we dwell on the qualities of the person and neglect the law of the office to which we elect our representatives. In addition, we frequently elevate individual conscience above the state's authority, without considering the state's right to rule within the sphere of its own competence and in accordance with the law of the land. In the case of capital punishment we ask how one person can have the right to take the life of another, without considering that in office the magistrate does not act simply on the basis of his person. However, the idea of office teaches that in whatever station we find ourselves, when we act according to the norm of our calling, it is God's promise that it is He who is acting through us and our work. This is how He has chosen to continue to work in the world.

We must admit, as Rev. Sietsma does, that in times past the idea of office was subverted in authoritarian and elitist ways. Paganism has had its caste systems and principles of natural superiority and inferiority. Man's dominion over creation has degenerated into some men dominating others. This appeared in the medieval view that reality is hierarchically ordered from lower to highest in a great chain of being, and has been reflected in the hierarchical structure of human institutions, including the church with its mutually exclusive classes of clergy and laity.

We now live in times, as Rev. Sietsma alerts us, which threaten exactly the opposite subversion of office. In modern times, especially since the French Revolution, traditional pagan and Christian authoritarian notions have been rejected. It is strongly denied that human beings are by nature different and unequal. With the rejection of authority from on high, there also came the rejection of the belief that the human exercise of authority over other human beings is rooted in the nature of things. The Enlightenment gospel, which led to the French Revolution, proclaimed that human beings are all created equal. Equality then came to be viewed as uniformity.

Thus, modern humanism begins with a critical, suspicious attitude toward authority, and toward the idea of office and official calling in life. With respect to the question of authority, this negative, critical modern spirit has totally transformed the idea of the "person." In earlier times, *personae* were thought to be the various roles and identities the human being carries in life. Each role of the "person" was thought *to represent* and mirror one important side of the individual's life.

As in the ancient theatre, the *persona* was a mask. In classical drama, as the players don their different masks, the masks of all the players taken together represent to the audience different sides of personhood, the different sides of human life. The "within" in man was thought to come to expression in his life's tasks and roles.

Quite the contrary view of the person has emerged in the modern period. The person today is viewed as an internal center of consciousness that is essentially non-present to the world outside. Hence, in the modern theatre, the various roles that players take or masks that they don do not so much (re)present the person as hide him. The word "mask," acquiring a negative connotation, has come to indicate how roles, positions, and identities are things behind which persons hide themselves and escape reality. In the modern theatre the *persona* inauthenticates the person and is thus suspect. Far from representing the person's many sides, the conventional roles are masks that conceal the real identity of persons. A prime example of this view of "office" is presented in Olaf Hartmann's *The Holy Masquerade* and is taken to the extreme in Camus' *The Stranger*.

Therefore, to revive proper thinking about "office," we

must work at heightening our consciousness of the Reformed faith in general. This means first of all that we must see that the exercise of authority of office ought not to be grounded in the nature of things, in human qualities and abilities. Against the ancients and pagans, Rev. Sietsma argues, we must maintain that the right of humans to exercise authority one over another is not based on the supposed natural superiority of some and the supposed natural inferiority of others. By nature we all stand immediately before God; thus, no human being has the right, *by created nature*, to exercise authority over any other human being.

Modernism must also be opposed with the idea of office. Modernism realizes that no human being has the right to exercise authority over others *by nature*, but it concludes from this that by *nature* every person is essentially the same and that office is at best a functional idea. Hence modernism replaces the concept of difference with the concept of sameness, the notion of equity with the idea of equality; whoever has the ability has the right to rule. Today modernism attempts to abolish even the most fundamental difference between persons given in creation, the difference between man and woman. With the abandonment of this created difference, the fabric of society threatens to come apart, for on it is based family and marriage and on these institutions the order of society itself depends.

In the church this modern idea of equality has often lead to the idea that all have the right to hold office and that the distinction between laity and special officers is arbitrary. Especially in Anabaptist circles, one hears it said that if before God all are officebearers in a general spiritual sense, then that fact should determine the order of things in the church.

However, as Rev. Sietsma shows so well, the fact that all believers are called to serve does not define the offices and stations in the various areas of life. We are indeed all called to service, but the question is *how* and *where*. In every area of life we are called to direct unto God, through our neighbor, whatever

God has ordered to be done. This service on God's behalf, however, does not specify the structure of how God and our neighbor are to be served; it only sets the right spiritual direction of whatever specific office or area we find ourselves in. For office is always as Rev. Sietsma points out, "service of God *in a specific work*" (emphasis mine) (p. 55). The directive does not specify the means.

Thus, even those who exercise rulership authority over persons, such as kings over their citizens and employers over their employees, should do so according to the God-ordained law of their office. Kings are called to serve *as rulers*, employers to serve *as masters*, citizens to serve *as subjects*, and employees to serve *as laborers*. The fact of "service" in each and every one of these cases neither undoes nor defines the nature of the specific office in which the service of God and neighbor is performed. The directive to serve is uniform in every calling and area of life. But since it is a directive, it does not determine the shape of the various offices. The directive defines and sets the spirit that must pervade the specific task, whatever it be. But the specific task is defined by God according to the orderly arrangement of things He established in the beginning.

Office, then, is service indeed, but always service in a specific work. Moreover, service, the general believing service to which we are all called as prophets, priests and kings, does not conflict with the special offices. Nor, for that matter, does the general office undo the need for special offices by redefining their shape on the basis of some leveling principle, as the Anabaptists and Donatists supposed. It is for this reason that the Reformers self-consciously emphasized *both* universal priesthood *and* the necessity of special office-holding in the church without any sense of tension between the two. Moreover, they did this not because they had not yet matured to a full abandonment of Catholic authoritarianism—as Anabaptist historiography alleges—but because in reality, and in the biblical view revised by the Reformers, no tension exists. In fact, in the biblical vision, universal priesthood and special office cannot exist without each other—any more than there is redemption without creation. If, then, we sense tension and inconsistency, it is because *we* have transformed the idea of universal priesthood into a structure-defining notion of general office-sharing and have thus fallen prey to the common Anabaptist, Donatist, and modern personalist collapse of norms into directives, creation into redemption, law into gospel. We no longer know how to think institutionally in a positive, principled manner.

Against ancient patriarchicalism, authoritarianism, and hierarchicalism, as well as against modern uniformism (Anabaptist and secular), we must maintain that humans do not exercise authority over one another *because* of principle, nor do they lack the right to exercise authority over one another *because* everyone is the same. As Rev. Sietsma reminds us, being the biotic source of my children does not authorize me to exercise authority over them, nor does being physically stronger, for even when I become less strong than they are, my authority does not cease. So too in the realm of political life, insight does not mean the right to hold office; nor for that matter does the having of great power warrant the state's right to rule. Similarly, having gifts in the church does not imply and bring with it the right to hold office. Just as in politics might does not make right, so in the church, talents do not entail rulership authority.

There is much confusion in Christian circles about the relationship of talents and gifts on the one hand to office and authority on the other. It has been suggested that talents are given for carrying out specific tasks. So the existing gifts determine who should do what in the community. In this view, talents and gifts precede office and authority. On the basis of the universal priesthood of all believers, everyone should either discharge or be able to discharge tasks in the institutional church according to his or her abilities. Reflecting this mentality, a pastor of a small Reformed denomination in North

America recently said this: "The office of all believers has been forgotten . . . we still cling to the structures of the past, still fearful to stand in the freedom of Christ. Elders cannot bless the congregation; believers cannot administer the sacraments, and women cannot pastor."

But what is forgotten here is that God has provided *an orderly way* in which to serve in the world. God has chosen the ways in which He and our neighbor should be served. Far from being a consequence of having gifts, office is that delegated and limited authority God has apportioned to each area of life. Thus, as Rev. Sietsma says: "The right to office does not inhere in human qualities . . . (but) rests in the sovereign disposition of the Lord God alone" (p. 34). Far from being the basis of office and authority, gifts are the necessary but not sufficient qualifications for leadership. The ungifted should not serve in the specific offices, generally speaking, but this in no way establishes that the gifted have the right to serve, and that office is merely the way in which, operationally, we make fullest use of their talents—no more than that having the power to do something means that the state thereby has the right to do it! What we *can* do should never be confused with what we *ought* to do.

We could go on in our review of this important aspect of Reformed faith and practice, for we have only highlighted those dimensions of Sietsma's teaching that are particularly relevant to our situation. There is much more, all of it worth our while. We can hope that Sietsma's simple essay will give the Christian community greater insight into that pattern of behavior established by God among men whereby He has chosen to be served as we serve our fellow man.

Henry Vander Goot

Foreword

"Office" has been at the heart of the age-old spiritual struggle of the human race in the various areas of life. Unfortunately, the idea of office has often been repressed for the sake of an institution or a strong and able person; worst of all people have fallen under the spell of powerful organizations or great leaders, without rightly discerning the question of office involved.

In many nations, revolutionary sentiment has collided with the official order, both parties working to their own advantage, and ignorant of the concept of office. In church affairs it has been the domination of the hierarchy or the triumph of the enthusiast leader, the extremes of clericalism and montanism, which have damaged our sense of office and official relationships. However, rebellion against the abuse of offices does not restore the office, but merely ameliorates a given situation. Revolution does not speak to the principial issues concerning office.

It must be remembered that office is the only justification and the proper limitation of any human exercise of power and authority. Except by virtue of his office, no one has a natural right to rule over any creaturely form of life. We owe no obedience to any human beings except inasmuch as they are office-bearers. And it is the office itself which limits the human office-bearer's exercise of authority. God alone is absolute; all human authority is by its very nature limited. The idea of an absolute authority *on earth* contradicts the idea of the absolute sovereignty of God.

All of the offices which govern human life limit one another. It is the ordering of the offices alongside of one another that protects against the transgression of the boundaries of office. Thus, the offices ordained by God to regulate human life are the foundation of societal connections and relationships.

The exercise of authority does not, then, depend on the condition or power of an organization or institution, nor on the gifts or stature of a given person. Rather, the exercise of authority depends on the appointment to an office, or the giving of a commission, and on the acknowledgment and acceptance of that office and commission. Moreover, the centrality of commission and delegated authority also pertains in situations where offices evolve naturally, such as in the family and in inherited rulership, and even in those situations where an office is occupied unrighteously.

In the whirlpool of revolutionary agitation, or in the reversals of reaction, this idea of office is forgotten. Then the masses waver before the bold action or ruthless word. Right relations and clear consciousness of task and authority become clouded.

Not only does this confusion occur outside of the Christian community; it also occurs among those who confess Christ. Ostensibly Christians have some convictions about office, especially about ecclesiastical office, which is still highly regarded among us. (I shall deal with it only in the context of our subject as a whole.) Moreover, Christians know about office in political life; nations have found their most serious and informed citizens among those who, being faithful to God, also yield to His office-bearers. Even office in the context of family is honored among Christians according to God's command. Such reverence for office yields good fruit.

But among Christians, too, there is much confusion, for this principle, which should rule all of life, is not fully understood. The spirit of our time influences many Christians, either by sweeping them along or by arousing them to reaction.

For the following reasons, then, we shall take a more careful look at this topic: (1) because the idea of office has a central significance that extends to the whole of a Christian's life; (2) because Christians are exposed to spiritual infections from the world in which they live; and, finally, (3) because so few Christians know what richness this dimension of God's will and ordinance holds for them.

The Scriptural Data

We shall begin by collecting from Scripture some data concerning the idea of office. We will begin then by demonstrating that the basic elements of the idea of office are revealed to us in Scripture.

We should first of all note that the word "office" is scarcely to be found in our traditional English translations of the Bible (except for the King James Version). Neither kingship, priesthood, or prophecy is called an "office." Nor are the tasks of apostle, evangelist, bishop, teacher, elder, or deacon referred to as offices. In the whole of the New Testament we have only the example of Acts 1:20, where reference is made to the "office of bishop."

Old Testament

In the Old Testament this term designates all kinds of functions besides those we have in mind when we use the term "office." For example, priests and Levites, who are divided into definite groups, are called "officials" because of their position. Some, however, were singers; others porters. Sometimes even the task of chief cook is called an "office." Yet elsewhere, "office" indicates the assigned task of a priest in his priestly service according to a specified time, such as the temple service.

In many Old Testament passages the work indicated by

"office" approaches what we would call the task of an official; sometimes it is associated with the work of judges. We might use the word "chief" or "supervisor." But always there is a certain authority implicit in the mandate. The term "office" could never be used for any work that is undertaken on *personal* initiative.

Now, as we expected, this investigation of the use of the word office in Scripture hardly advances the discussion. Nonetheless, even at this point we can in connection with the use see that there is always presumed to be a certain authority in actions undertaken in the framework of an office. To better understand the biblical conception of office, we need to examine those words in Scripture that are often rendered by the term "office."

First we should take the Hebrew word *pakad*, which is sometimes translated "census" or "review." It also often means "supervision" or "oversight," especially in the temple. Finally, it is often translated "visitation," whether for deliverance or chastisement. The basic idea is thus "supervision," "control," "inspection," or "superintendence."

Furthermore, we have the Hebrew word *aman*, sometimes translated "office," as in the temple-service. This term is related to our "Amen." Thus it means "firmness" or "immovability." Therefore, it is also used for the "faithfulness" of God or of men, and thereby becomes closely related to the idea of "truth" in Scripture.

The most important word for our purposes, however, is the Hebrew term *abhad*, which usually means "labor," or "service," as in I Chronicles 6:32, where it is sometimes translated "priestly office." When the terms "labor" and "service" are used, they are used in almost all of their possible meanings: the work of God but also the labor of man; temple service or the general priestly or levitical service. In addition, this term is used as the standing expression for service of the Lord.

Of this Hebrew term, the form *ebhed* indicates the person who does the work or engages in the service—a man's slave or a king's servant. It can indicate a polite form of service to others, or a form of reverence to God. But above all, it means "servant of God." In the Old Testament one of the most significant expressions for "believer," especially one appointed by God for the execution of a specific task, is *ebhed Jahweh*, or servant of the Lord.

Ebhed Jahweh is used to indicate in general that one is subject to the Lord; however, it serves primarily to indicate the special relation created by God between Himself and His people for obedient service commensurate with His graciousness. Both Israel as a whole and faithful individual Israelites are identified as such "servants of the Lord." Those expressly so named in the Old Testament are servants like Abraham, Joshua, Job, and David, and what is implied is that the Lord has bound this specific servant to Himself and His service by a special mandate.

Thus the name is used even for the kings of Babylon (Jeremiah 25:9, 27:6, and 43:10) and for angels (Job 4:18). But it is usually a term of honor reserved for a human being which sets him in special relation to God, a relation of service in God's redemptive plan for His people. The prophets are so designated (II Kings 9:7; Jeremiah 7:25, 25:4, 26:5, 29:19), and Moses is as well (Deuteronomy 34:5; Joshua 1:1, etc.).

Very significantly this name (*ebhed Jahweh*) is used in a very special way in Isaiah's prophecies (Ch. 40ff), where the coming and work of the Messiah, the anointed of the Lord, is described. In this context He is constantly referred to by the name "Servant of the Lord," or "My Servant."

Now we can better take our bearings concerning the concept of office in the Old Testament. We note first of all that in the Old Testament, there is, in the forefront, the special office, established and described by ordinances. The liturgical office is particularly important. This agrees with the nature of the old dispensation, which was first of all highly ceremonial in its foreshadowing of the New Covenant. The second characteristic is what Paul emphasizes when he calls Israel a *child*, thereby underscoring the legal nature of Israel's worship. All of Israel's life was hedged about by commandments and precepts; every relation was seen in terms of a sharply defined task and a precisely delimited calling.

In this context, an office was a mandate and a gift which made possible the service of God. A doorkeeper was not merely figuratively but literally an office-bearer in the house of God. Of course, the idea of general office was not absent in the Old Testament period, as we shall see. But that deeper, more general meaning of office was hidden behind specific, more superficial "offices," as one might expect in the old dispensation.

New Testament

Although the specific term "office" seldom appears in the New Testament, an important place is reserved for the special office. For example, in the apostolic letters we repeatedly meet with exhortations to reverence authorities in the civil, social, and familial domains. Ecclesiastical office is dealt with in particular; in various places, institutions, functioning, requirements, and powers of special offices in the church are discussed and defined.

In this respect the difference from the Old Testament is noticeable. Since the ceremonial service has passed away, the spiritual background and deeper religious sense of office comes to the fore in the New Testament.

Significantly, in the New Testament nearly all the offices, but especially the ecclesiastical, are designated by the general concept of "servanthood." Only the deacon has retained the nomenclature of servanthood to designate his office (*diakonos*); the other office-bearers are variously called elders, supervisors, shepherds, teachers, etc. However, the general or class term for all the offices is "servant," or "servanthood," and the general task is "serving." Hence, in the New Testament as in the Old, we seem to arrive at the description of office as service, service to God and to one's neighbor.

Already in the Old Testament we saw that office must be accompanied by good order, by the placing of something under supervision, by the assignment of a particular task and definite authority, and by an appointment of someone to a specific position, an appointment made by a higher authority, ultimately God Himself. The Old and New Testaments together teach us that the deeper and basic relationship can be expressed by the term "service" and related words. The relationship of service can appear in every context. But the most special context is the service of the Lord God in the whole breadth and extent of His work.

Service of God can mean the formal service of worship; in fact, it can mean obedience that is still only external. But service takes on its deepest, fullest, and most fitting sense when it is used to signify all that one is and has, put at the disposal of the Lord God as commissioner.

Ultimately, then, the Old and New Testaments are in full agreement. The New Testament concept of "service" is many-faceted and well-developed, for it needed to be well-taught. In the Greek world into which the Gospel was first brought, "service" was held in low regard and even disdained. It was the work of a slave, a being of the lowest esteem. The Greeks thought that a free man, whose life's task was the development of his own personality, was too noble for "service." The Greek ideals were "ruling," and "striving to be perfect," notions that contrast sharply to the idea of "service."

Even the Jews had become estranged from the Old Testament idea of service. They mouthed the idea of service of God and called themselves "His servants." But in their conception, there was little left of the ideal of being at God's disposal, of being strong in humility. Among the Old Testament covenant people there was little left of the sense of being born a "servant-slave."

The humble service of one's neighbor hardly appealed to the proud Pharisees and Sadducees. Their service was limited to the group or clan. Moreover, service of God had become largely a form of bartering with God done by a "chosen" people who had become smug and self-satisfied.

In the face of this, the Lord Jesus proclaimed the fear of the Lord, a service synonymous with faith and being a child of the heavenly Father. In the New Testament the full meaning of service emerges, including the idea of office, as the term "service" is used for the service of God.

Chapter 1

Office Lost and Restored

We must distinguish carefully between the Office of Man and the Office of the Son of Man. "Service" has to do with man's task before God. All service rendered to persons or to any authority among men both reflects and issues from that service to which God called man and for which He created him. In a certain sense every creature (in addition to man) is created to serve God, and does actually serve Him. But we cannot therefore regard every creature as an "office-bearer." The biblical concept of "service" does not come into its own until applied to man.

We might also be inclined to include angels in a class with man. They too are servants or messengers of God. Indeed, Lord's Day 49 of the Heidelberg Catechism interprets the third petition of the Lord's Prayer ("Thy will be done") in such a way that faithful angels serve as examples to follow in the fulfillment of our office and the execution of our calling.

But the Catechism does not mean that angels have received offices and callings in the same sense as man has. On the contrary, the Catechism speaks only of *our* office and calling. The angels are indeed faithful servants; but in their service they possess no creaturely independence, initiative, or self-action. The angels are ministering spirits sent to do the work of God, even to serve the "heirs of salvation" (Hebrews 1:14). God appoints man and man alone as His servant and office-bearer. The

Lord gifts man with a mandate, to be fulfilled with self-conscious and deliberate choice, with independent initiative. On this creaturely self-action hinges the future of man and of all things created to be subordinate to man.

Scripture calls this responsibility of man both service and administration. To serve in office is to administer God's care and love to His creatures. The entire creation is dependent for its future on whether man will serve or not. This relationship to God called "office" is more than a relationship inherent in the nature of things or in the nature of man. Nor is it inherent in the idea that progeny are dependent upon their source or in the idea that God created man as a naturally higher or greater creature than the animals.

Man exists in official relationship to God. He represents the whole human race, and the entire creation made subject to him. Because of what he will do or leave undone in that capacity, the entire creation will be either blessed or cursed. God's relationship to man is the crux of the matter; the relationship of office has been *ordained* by God. *God has by His will made the assignment and issued the mandate. Only because of God are these things the way they are.*

Thus, two elements in the idea of office come to the forefront: (1) the idea that man is charged with responsibility, though granted a certain relative independence vis-à-vis God; and (2) the idea that the essence of office depends on the divine mandate.

First, man is charged with responsibility. When the work assigned to someone consists in no more than carrying out a blueprint for action, it is not possible to speak of responsible independence, and therefore it is really not accurate to speak of "office," unless the bearer of that office be in infancy, as was the case in many respects in ancient Israel.

Second, the official relationship is not inherent in the nature of things; *it exists by divine command.* This is an important point. Sometimes even Christians assume that official relations are rooted in the nature of things. They think that God has so connected the official and the natural that every natural relationship, or quality, or talent, or gift implies and warrants the bearing of office.

The office of fatherhood in the family is a good example. Every father possesses God-given authority as father. The mistake is to think that the father's authority and prerogative are based on the natural fact of propagation and procreation. Sometimes one hears the claim that the child owes respect to his father and mother because he owes his origin and existence, and thus everything, to them.

But such an argument misses the essence of the matter. For the ground of paternal authority lies not in the natural principle of procreation, but *in the appointment and will of God*. A father's authority over his children is rooted in nothing other than the decree of the Lord. By divine providence and orderly management, persons become parents of children. Every child should consequently show reverence, love and faithfulness to his parents. All this is so not by nature but by the good pleasure of God, who has *chosen* to rule children through the hands of the parents.

This is not hairsplitting, but the making of a distinction which touches the very basics of life. The reason for the exercise of any human office or authority can never be found in anything other than the will and ordinance of God, even though His will and ordinance often become discernible in the natural course of things and in natural relationships.

The Fall

Furthermore, we must carefully distinguish between our having been created and our having been given the special office of servants of God. It is, of course, not the case that God created man out of two separate parts, the human being on the one hand and man's function as office-bearer on the other. On the contrary, according to God's purpose, man as God's image-bearer comes into his own *only* when he accepts and executes his office as servant of the Lord.

Yet we must distinguish these two elements; otherwise, it will not be clear how man remained man even though his qualities and capabilities became defaced when he rejected his office and mandate. Furthermore, the two elements must be distinguished to keep clear how man can be reinstated in his office even though the renewal of God's image in man can never be complete and perfect.

We all know the story: man fell and thereby deprived himself of his original righteousness and holiness. In fact, all of his relationships, functions and gifts became distorted. And yet the image of God did not completely disappear, for man did not cease to be man.

Man, placed in the garden to serve God, and thus to find his fulfillment and whole sense of meaning in life, fell from his office when he turned against God. He began to live for himself according to a mandate of his *own*; actually he became a slave of the devil.

Service of the devil differs in kind from service of God. Of course, these two services differ in the sense that the former is deadly and the latter salutory, and they do both represent a kind of service. However, it is not the case that in both man surrenders his ability to do as he might choose.

When man serves God, he fulfills not only the will of God but his own will as well. As God's office-bearer, man does perfect justice to his own nature and character. Man comes into full being and self-hood only in loving and obedient relationship to God. This is how man was created in his original state of righteousness, and it remains fundamentally true even now.

In absolute contrast to godly service, in the service of satan, man is a slave. He does the will of satan, in conformity with his own *perverted* will and *corrupted* desire, and what he does subverts and destroys his own created self-hood and gifts. Sin is not only a transgression of the law of God, which leads to punishment, but it is also a calamity for man, whose good, created nature is destroyed by enslavement to the devil.

Slavery under the devil is nothing like office. Seeking independence, man fell from his official position of responsibility in the service of God and ended up under the tyranny of the evil one.

Of course, satan did not succeed in destroying man completely. Man is not a devil, full of conscious and deliberate hate for God. We believe, according to what we designate "common grace," that there are active in the world and in man many energies or powers of the Word and Spirit of God which prevent the transformation of all that God once created good into its very opposite. The Lord sees to it that the thoughts of the human mind, the affections of the human heart, and the works of the human hand still manifest His glory and the rich qualities of His creation. There remains on earth a rich form of human life, even where there is no regeneration of the heart and even where the grace of salvation has not been bestowed.

But the relationship of office has been broken. And so, even when fallen man does what is good in a general sense, he can not be said to do this in service of God, according to the divine mandate and for God's sake. This is what Scripture and the confessions mean when they say that man is not only inclined *by nature* to hate God and his neighbor, but also that he is incapable of performing any good.

This does not only mean that man will often break forth in hatred against God and his neighbor; it also means that what he does is not good until it is done in the relationship of office. Surely it was into an office that man was placed with his gifts and potentialities, and so it is only in that relationship that he can live a life well-pleasing to God. One way of articulating this difference is to say that the believer *intends* the deeds that he does and the words that he expresses to be to the glory of God; and that the unbeliever does not so *intend*.

A more appropriate way of saying this also illuminates the

idea of office more clearly. If by the word "intend" we mean that the believer lives unto the glory of God only when he "consciously" keeps God's glory before him, doing things as unto the Lord, we would be viewing the matter too narrowly. Similarly, we would be viewing the matter too narrowly if we maintained that the unbeliever reviles God only when he deliberately purposes to thwart the cause of the Lord and dishonor His name. Instead, we must look at the whole of a person's posture and position in life, which comes down to that person's attitude to and relationship with God.

Indeed, the unbeliever, the person not born again by the Holy Spirit, can never purpose or intend to be well pleasing to the Lord. When he acts deliberately, he always conflicts with God, though he may not always be conscious of his intentions or their consequences. The whole tenor of his life is set by his broken relationship to God.

A believer's intentions tend in the opposite direction. The believer intends to live to the praise of the Lord and to place himself in God's service. Of course, he speaks words and performs deeds which conflict with his calling and office as servant of the Lord. And there are also areas of life in which con sciousness does not determine his thinking, feeling, and acting.

Still we must say that the believer always serves the God of the covenant and is active in that service, whether he be a young child, an adult fast asleep, or a worker intent on work at hand, without conscious thoughts of God. In all these things, the believer does indeed serve God and glorifies His name. Why? Because he is an office-bearer. He is always and continually in office, for the office embraces the whole of life. Man is always involved in that office, provided he does not rebel against it. Accordingly, we can understand Paul's words about "doing all to the glory of God, whether we eat, drink, or whatever we do" (I Corinthians 10:31).

We can look for an illustration of the activity of an office-bearer in government service. He does not on every occasion in which he exercises his authority repeat his oath of office. For at all times in the exercise of his office he is under the oath he took in the beginning. So too, the believer *always* stands in office. All his acts are official acts, whether they be acts that honor or dishonor his office. *He is never neutral.*

Correlatively, the unbeliever's posture *always* remains that of an office-breaker, even when he does his utmost to do what is good as he judges it, even in his various religious activities. The fact that the Lord may take these deeds of the unbeliever and by His restraining and directing power turn them to His own glory does not change the unbeliever's position as office-bearer. The unbeliever does not perform his deeds for the glory of God. He does not perform them *in service*, not because he deliberately intends opposition to God's will, but because, not being in the true service of God, he stands diametrically opposed to God.

If we wish to understand the distortions sin has brought about, we must firmly maintain these two points. First, as man has rejected his office, his intentions, as we reflect upon them and as the Lord sees them, are always directed perversely. Second, unbelieving man continues to stand outside of the service of God. We might say he stands in service of himself and his ideals; more pointedly, we might say that he stands in service of satan.

So far we have illustrated that man's fall into sin was a fall from his office. Only restoration to that office can make possible genuine service of the Lord. We shall speak then of a restoration to office that finds its complement in regeneration, in which the restored office-bearer can again do what is required of him and can again will what he should will.

Chapter 2

Christ the Office-Bearer

The restoration of man to his rightful office has come into being in and through Christ. He is *the* office-bearer, the one and the first. By His fulfillment of office, it has been restored and returned to mankind.

Christ's great fulfillment of His office, is a fascinating topic; however, we must touch on it only briefly. When we say that Christ is the office-bearer, we think of Lord's Day 12 of the Heidelberg Catechism, which affirms that He is prophet, priest and king. Accordingly, we so distinguish the different aspects of His office. However, the offices of Christ are not separate, nor is the work of Christ exhausted in the fulfillment of these three. They are, in fact, three integrated aspects of the one office. We could not cite one action of Christ in which only one of the three would function independently. And we could cite more sides of the office than these three, for there are other official designations ascribed to Christ in Scripture.

It is highly significant that Scripture calls the Son of God the Christ, the Messiah, or the Anointed One without further mention of the specific tasks to which He was appointed. Those names signify the *full* work that He accomplished. Frequently one of those names is supplemented by a term such as Redeemer or Mediator, or, as Scripture itself puts it: Christ Jesus; the Annointed Jesus; the Savior. The name "the Christ of God" means the one anointed by God to be the bearer of the office.

In more recent times we often hear it said that the name "Christ" signifies the Man. But we would express this thought differently. He who is the Son of God from eternity became the Son of Man in time, the one who in the eternal Council of Peace made Himself available for the work of God. In the incarnation, the Word became man by being born of the Virgin Mary. He is thus the one who accepted the office of Mediator between God and man, officially entering into all those states which He as Son of Man and Surety for sinners had to enter in order to re-establish the office.

In the language of this discussion, we would say that Christ took the office of Covenant head, which man had lost, upon Himself. He became the new representative of the human race, the Second Adam. He accomplished all that the first Adam should have done in his office, and submitted Himself to what man should have undergone because of his profaning of the office. Two instances will help make the point.

The first is the baptism of Jesus in the Jordan. One might well wonder why it was possible that the pure and holy Jesus would undergo baptism for the remission of sins. Surely He could not have repented. The baptism of Jesus must, then, have been of a different character than ours.

It is frequently said that Jesus wanted to become like us in all things. Indeed, this is true. But the idea of office makes even more sense of this incident in the life of Jesus. He did not descend into the Jordan as the sinless man Jesus, and surely not as divine. No, Jesus Christ went down as office-bearer, as our representative, the one who had become the new head of the human race.

In that office, He indeed went down into the Jordan on our behalf, and in so doing was indeed viewed as a sinner before God. Thus baptism for repentance and the remission of sins could indeed make good sense for Him. He did not violate the normal sense of baptism; he did full justice to it. In His baptism, He stood before God as one weighed down with the burden of sin. Sin had to be destroyed through His death, foreshadowed by His baptism in the Jordan.

The second instance which illustrates the genuineness of Christ's fulfillment of human office is His uttering these words from the cross: "My God, My God, why hast Thou forsaken Me?" Neither in His divinity nor in His purity could Jesus have been forsaken by His Father. It was Jesus the office-bearer who suffered this estrangement. He who speaks this agony is the Mediator between God and man. Assuming that office as representative of the human race and accountable for its sinfulness, He entered into it fully and deeply. So, too, He was justly and righteously rejected by God. As our Guarantor, He assumed our obligations, even though as a person He was upright.

As office-bearer, Christ was the human being who performed all the work that man was to accomplish. Moreover, He bore all of the punishment for sin that man had to bear. Since He has not taken the office of man to be merely a model or example, but is rather man's covenant head and representative, He restores the office and maintains it for the entire human race. By His service, the service of man is restored. By His maintenance of the office, the office becomes restored, and man comes once again to stand before God in a right relationship. Whoever acknowledges God in Jesus receives the office and is able to assume the original service of obedience to God.

The Office Preserved

Much of what has just been said is widely accepted among Christians. What many ignore, however, is the fact that *every* office has been restored in Christ, and that every official mandate has its deepest *raison d'être* in Christ's fulfillment of man's office.

Here we touch on the question of common grace, which is somewhat related to our topic.

Some Christians insist that all the goodness God shows

toward man and creation comes from Christ's merit. They maintain that there can be no manifestation of God's mercy apart from the merit of Christ. If there were mercy apart from Christ's merit, so the argument goes, then God would be overlooking sin. In this general bridling of the pervasiveness of sin, there appears to be a certain "grace" outside of Christ.

Other Christians who also emphasize that only the elect partake of Christ, and who would reject the idea of two kinds of salvation would at the same time maintain that all kinds of blessings and gifts are given to the unregenerate apart from the saving work of Christ. These good things can be understood only as fruits of God's common grace. Common grace is not wholly unrelated to Christ's work, and yet there is a radical difference between the relationship of the regenerate and the unregenerate to Christ. So goes their argument.

The people still believe that good things in the world have some relation to the work of Christ; they believe that the restraining grace of God is part of the Lordship of Christ, and they believe that this grace serves the edification and completion of the body of Christ.

The central issue in this debate is the nature of fallen humanity. Is there in humanity a certain created goodness and beauty maintained through the fall, or did the fall mean such a complete breach with God that these "remnants" of goodness are not really remnants but favors of God that flow to humanity from the work of Christ?

When our confessions speak of "remnants" of goodness and truth, they actually mean that by God's restraining power, human nature was not totally destroyed, nor was creation turned into a hell. The gifts of creation were far from revoked after the fall; in fact, favors and gifts from God preceded even the first announcement of coming salvation (Genesis 3:15). The "remnants" found in fallen man are thus indeed "remnants" in that they were not created anew. Rather, by protective preservation they were maintained.

On the other hand, the preservation of these "remnants" of God's good work has its deepest foundation in the official work of Christ, even though the work and proclamation of Christ came later in history. To be sure, man could only know about preservation and recreation *after* the Lord had spoken. However, God the Lord had established Christ by His will from all eternity and could thus cause the fruit of Christ's work to ripen before He came in the flesh to accept His office—in fact, even before the promise was first given in the garden.

Moreover, the fact that common grace was present before the first promise was given does not split common grace away from Christ. Nor does the connection with Christ detract from the fact that the fruits of common grace are, at least in part, a *remnant* of the work of God in creation. Thus there need be no conflict between the idea of "remnants" preserved in creation and the idea of a complete breach with God and the restorative work which can take place only in Christ.

Thus, no person born of Adam, nor even Adam himself, ever perished *absolutely* under God's wrath even though the relationship between God and man was *completely* broken and corrupted. Man continued living and working, bearing and inheriting the blessings of both general and particular grace—to use the well-known distinction—solely because God *had already* elected Christ and in Him the Christ Incarnate. Even in the very moment in which man broke relationship with God, it was already restored; in promise and in principle, the Second Adam *immediately* took over the work of the first Adam. In this way, God made possible every relationship of service and blessing, the gifts of His mercy and grace, and the labor and life-redeeming action which He blesses.

This is how we would explain the mystery of an office instituted and maintained by God when the person bearing the office has not yet been incorporated into Christ. The office itself was redeemed by Christ's fulfillment of it, and thus it remains an integrating element in the life of humanity. The time will come when *every* office will be filled by members of the new redeemed humanity. As yet this is not the case. For now, the office as rescued and preserved can be borne by the unregenerate, even though the office is maintained by the work of Christ.

We have now a most wonderful and beautiful situation. The goodness God created when He charged man with an office and a calling has been salvaged from the fall. There remain in the world all kinds of offices maintained by God, even when they are only partially exercised by man. For the Christian, in whom office and person can be harmonized, the complete service of God is in principle restored. But in the general sense, too, office remains. On the one hand, God commands that the bearer execute the office in obedience to God's law, on the other hand God allows the office to be assumed by those who do not recognize God as ultimate authority, who therefore live in conflict with the true service of God. But even in the latter situation, the office remains an office given by God, and it must be acknowledged as such by those who bow before God's Word, even though the bearer of that office be disobedient and rebellious.

To sum up: man has lost the office and Christ has restored it. But those remaining in apostasy have not as yet been removed from their official positions. The time of grace is extended so that restoration of office might be a genuine *re*-creation and *re*-stitution of what was given in the beginning. God intends to re-establish His rule among and from out of the very humanity He created.

In this interim in which we live, the office, wherever and however represented, must be fully maintained as a continuation of God's creation and as part of the restored order of things. There exists among men a general office, allowing us to speak of a common mandate.

More particularly, this order of God appears in the offices whereby the various spheres of human existence are ruled. In them the divine preservation and promise of restoration speaks loud and clear. For this reason Scripture places heavy emphasis on the office even when the person who occupies it is far from obedient to God. One of the best biblical examples of this is the attitude of David toward King Saul. When the first king of Israel was already rejected by God—and David knew it—David nonetheless continued to recognize Saul as the anointed of the Lord, and refused to take his life. In this we witness a reverence for an office that God has not yet abandoned and from which David does not consider Saul yet ejected.

The epistle of Jude provides an even stronger example. We have pictured a contest between the archangel Michael and the devil over the body of Moses. The writer says that even Michael did not dare bring an accusation against the devil, but rather left the judgment to God Himself. Clearly this was because the devil in his office was still an archangel, though he had himself fallen. He had not yet been stripped of his official glory and cast into hell.

Chapter 3

Office in the Various Spheres

We have seen that the official order of things is maintained by God for the greater blessing of human society. In fact, God-given office is both the only justification for and the only boundary of human authority. It is the only disposition of human relationships in which they are secure against both anarchy and tyranny. This point deserves more explication.

We have already said that office involves institutional authority granted by God; it is an appointment by God to a position endowed with majesty and authority. Now this must be taken in as broad a sense as possible, for office extends over all of human life, embracing man's place in the entire context of creation and the covenant. In other words, the relations of office order all of human life. Moreover, this disposition of things is the only fundamental and enduring order because it is inherent in the nature of things as created by God.

The question always arises, though: How are abilities, gifts and talents related to office? How many children aren't disobedient to their parents, finding it difficult to honor them duly because they do not respect their parents' abilities and wisdom? Measuring their parents by their own personal standards, children find them wanting, and then take the liberty to disobey.

Moreover, how many parents aren't there who rule their children with strength and ability, wielding power and punish-

ment, but who fail to understand that their authority is not
ultimately theirs, but has been given to them by God. Such a
situation sooner or later ends in catastrophe, for the power of
physical or moral superiority will finally prove too limited to
keep children in line. At some point or another a child will likely
become stronger, wiser, or more educated than his parents, and
then the parent-child relationship based on power will collapse.
In some cases things are still held together by familial affection,
but the bonds are fragile, for they are not rooted in an
understanding of the basic relationship. The fundamental relationship should remain intact even when the child has matured
beyond the measure of his parents, for it is a relationship of office which God has established.

A second example comes from the sphere of government.
Often church leaders, teachers, professors, or managers of the
economy understand the issues close to them much better than
do the elected officials of the nation. For this reason, it is
argued, the non-political areas of life should be left to the supervision of those who know most about them. The government's
responsibility not to interfere is thought to be grounded in the
superior wisdom and insight of these leaders.

Now it is quite true that government officials are not endowed with the wisdom to supervise a whole multifaceted society. Yet this is not the issue at stake. If it were the basic issue, we
would be able to ensure a healthy society if we could but train a
class of political officials who would thus be capable of governing wisely all the various sectors of society.

However, thinking along these lines conflicts with the
created order of things. For the Lord has limited all those in
authority on earth to their own spheres of competence.
Transgression of those boundaries established by God leads in-
variably to destruction.

Each of the various spheres has its own structure, and an
office in one sets limits to offices in the others. When one office
infringes on another, it is a violation of office as instituted by

God. For this reason, all illegitimate interference must be resisted by means appropriate to the office being defended.

The nurture of children belongs to the office of parents; the management of schools to the office of educators; the practice of science to the office of those appointed to that sphere. Moreover, the state has the calling and right by virtue of its office to supervise society, to remove abuses, to restrain the lawless, and to protect the weak from the strong. It follows, then, that in God's creation no person or institution has unlimited dominion, or is safe from possible deposition.

It also follows that no one finds the norms for his actions within himself. Therefore, the exercise of authority must always be in a leading and guiding mode and must never degenerate into tyranny. It is God who holds absolute authority over His creation; all men are subordinate and subject to God's laws. God has bestowed upon each sphere of human life certain rules for living, a certain order of things. These laws naturally propel man in a certain direction as man exercises his authority or gifts within a particular sphere.

We are discussing the authority that one person exercises over another. In principle all human beings are alike before God, their Creator. There is nothing inherent in the nature of one human being that he should rule over others, or that one race should have dominion over another. There is no natural right of one group to exercise authority over another. All authority belongs purely to office. Some exercise authority over others because of the providential direction of God. This authority is sustained because God gives the office, and this authority is also limited by its official character, for the Lord has subordinated one human being to another strictly for the good of the subordinate, and not because he is inferior or required by nature to obey.

This does not mean, of course, that specific gifts have nothing to do with a person's qualifications for leadership, nor does it mean that lack of gifts necessarily disqualifies another for office. The right to office does not inhere in human qualities, no more than the obligation of subordinates to obey stems from some alleged inferiority. Authority rests in the sovereign disposition of the Lord God alone.

This idea that all people are fundamentally alike is sometimes called democracy. In the name of democracy, it is sometimes argued that investing a particular office with authority is undemocratic. But this way of thinking is misguided. One can, of course, make proper use of the term "democracy." But when the term is taken to mean that the people themselves are the seat of authority, the idea of office is destroyed as it is transformed into the idea of the mandate of the masses. This idea contradicts the truth that God alone is sovereign and that no one may establish norms for his life by himself, or is a law unto himself.

Moreover, the concept of democracy is often related to the French Revolution, whether this is historically correct or not. It might be proposed that the slogan of "equality" used in the Revolution spoke of a truth very much like the principial notion of equality with which we have been working. But this is not the case. On the contrary, the revolutionary notion of equality is the equality of the masses, of innumerable individuals who possess the right to rule and who will not hear of the notion of official authority.

When we speak of human equality, we have something totally different in mind: a certain equality *before God*. Every person has the possibility of exercising authority in office and every person has the duty to obey those in office. We must keep clear the difference between the biblical idea of equality and office and the Revolutionary idea of equality and authority.

What we must maintain on Christian grounds is this: The special office in any sphere does not exist to give honor or privilege to a class of superior persons. On the contrary, the special office exists to provide order and authority in human society so that it may function according to the ordinances of God.

Because there is no creature on earth who could exercise authority over man, the office-bearer is taken from among human beings themselves. Office-bearers are necessary because human life is distorted and immature. Men and women are not able to live in harmony nor to honor societal relationships without guidance and authority.

In a certain sense, then, the special office exists because of sin—not simply for the bridling of sin, but for the guidance and direction of creatures who have not yet come to their maturity. Therefore, the more mature and wise must lead the inexperienced and immature. And even where this discrimination can not be made, the office represents justice, wisdom, and experience.

We want to stress too that obedience to the office is never blind obedience. The whole community's wisdom, sense of justice, and energy of mind and spirit ought to be incorporated into its leadership in every area of life. To insist on reasonable popular input in political life is not false democratism, for office does not mean autocratic rule, but rather, order and guidance. Those who exercise guidance shall profit from the knowledge and constructive abilities present in the community. Not every human desire or expression of human will and ego has its place, but important contributions can be made for the good of the body by those who do not occupy the special office. In other words, the special office is supported and limited by the official position of each member of the community.

Objective and Subjective

Before we turn to a discussion of the various spheres of life, we should attend to one more matter, the matter of official position and inherent ability, which sometimes appears as the matter of objective appointment to office and subjective sense of calling. What is the relationship between these two?

To begin our discussion, we might consider the case of a person called to office who declares that he feels called by the congregation and therefore by the Lord Himself. However, often he does not really understand the idea of office. In fact, many chosen to office and many who respect and obey those so chosen evaluate the matter almost exclusively in terms of competence, and end up confused.

When a brother chosen for eldership or the deaconate considers only the question of whether he feels capable of the office he may, in modesty, quite easily conclude that he lacks the proper ability. On the other hand, someone who is presumptuous and immodest may conclude that the call to office is an honor appropriately accorded to him. To exacerbate the problem, the acceptance or decline of a call is often made dependent on such self-evaluation.

Of course, ability matters. No one can deny that in the Lord's church it is important that those called to office really have the necessary gifts to function well in the office. But two things must not be forgotten: first, that even if there is a brother in the congregation with greater gifts than the brother chosen, the latter man has been elected to the office, and that he must be acknowledged by himself and by others; and second, the judgment concerning ability does not rest with the person himself, nor with independent observers, but rests in the office. In the case of ecclesiastical election, it resides in the consistory, which has been called to give guidance in this matter.

As regards the acceptance of office, every confessing male member may be nominated and chosen to special office. Each such member, when chosen in a lawful manner, should accept the office as assigned to him by God. He may, however, turn down the office if he can show a call to another office which would suffer from the combination. He may also refuse the office if he can show that another office he holds has prior consideration.

Therefore it should not be the case that someone accepts a call because he feels capable of the office. Rather, having been called by the congregation and as such by God, the person chosen accepts the office in spiritual obedience, expecting that the Lord will increase his ability not by any miraculous strokes, but according to His faithful promise.

The implications of this illustration are far-reaching. Indeed, the issue of the subjective and the objective accepting of office, of inner ability and official calling, touches nearly the whole of human life. During the time of the Reformation, there were conflicts over this issue. The Roman Catholic Church represented the objectivist view in which the institution and the hierarchy of the church were considered infallible. The office was assumed to carry with it the Spirit of God, just as the sacrament was assumed to embody grace in an almost physical sense.

By contrast the Anabaptist and Humanist views border on subjectivism. Anabaptists view man pessimistically; Humanists, optimistically. Both subjectivisms begin with man, man as capable by nature or man rendered capable by regeneration. Eventually this subjectivism gives birth to the idea of revolution, just as the divinization and legitimization of the institution is born of the Catholic view. Both objectivists and subjectivists, however, destroy the idea of office at its very heart.

Surely the norm for the office is to be sought neither in the objective, that is, in the organization apart from the office-bearer, nor in subjective, internal experience. Rather it is to be sought in the law of God, and in the daily working out of office which seeks to obey and maintain God's law. Office is the central matter, the firm foundation. Prerequisite for the proper functioning of the office is what we may call in the broadest sense the inspiration of the Holy Spirit. But in any case, the ground of the relationship between office-bearer and subject is the office and the official appointment.

Office and Power

We have taken care to establish, on Scriptural grounds, how the idea of office entails reverence for and obedience to the office-bearer, which is not exactly the same as mere acknowledgment of the power of rulers or ruling bodies. In the sphere of political life this difference appears most prominently, though somehow it is often overlooked.

It seems that in recent years respect for authority is making a come-back. We can take heart about this; better consequences will flow from it than from undercutting and despising authority.

However, something is still lacking here: such recognition of authority is no genuine victory over the revolutionary principle, for it is not a genuine recognition of office and a corresponding obedience to it. Pressure in the direction of authority comes from nearly every aspect of public life. But people differ vastly on the question of who is to possess the authority and by whom this authority is to be given. Some wish authority to be concentrated in a leader, one strong man who can centralize and make his authority effective. Of course, he would have help and advisors, but he would be ultimately responsible for the course of events. Power and authority would thus reside in his person; he would be sovereign.

Directly opposed to this view of authority is the view which invests ''the people''—a conglomerate of individuals—with all authority. The end result is a dictatorship by the party or group in majority.

Both views believe that ultimate authority resides in the will of the human being, whether individually or collectively conceived. For this reason, on the basis of Scriptural principles, there is no fundamental or absolute difference among democracy, aristocracy, oligarchy, and monarchy. A great difference does exist between biblical principles and the root of all these political conceptions.

The underlying belief common to all these political points of view is the idea that the person (individually or collectively conceived) is the foundation of authority in the state. The idea of office has no place in any of these systems. The Scriptural position, however, makes the idea of office central. We must view our governors and rulers as office-bearers, or we are in a wrong relationship to them. No single human being has the natural right to rule over another except in his capacity as office-bearer. Moreover, no one is under obligation to obey anyone else except on account of the office that the one above him occupies.

Now it may seem that this idea of office is just another way of establishing a foundation for traditional authority in our society. Some people might think that all they need to do is to include in their political programs some acknowledgment that kings rule by God's grace and that God Himself is finally Sovereign. But we submit that their unity with us would be only apparent. Their reasons for rejecting revolutionary philosophy are not ours. The idea of office does not come into its own when we recognize in theory that those who govern us govern by the grace of God. On the contrary, the idea of office demands a change in our practice; certain practical consequences flow forth from it.

One such consequence is that we honor, obey, respect, and support bearers of the office, even when they are not the representatives of our choice. If we hurl defiant and dishonoring words at our office-bearers, if we think it right to advance our own views by undermining the authority of those who have been clothed with the office of government by God's providence, then we have not understood the idea of office. We are still under the spell of personalism, of glorying and trusting in persons when we applaud and obey because a certain person whom we regard highly has been elected and when we withhold approval and genuine obedience because someone else has been elected. Such attitudes cannot be harmonized with the idea of honor due our office-bearers as taught by the Heidelberg Catechism (Lord's Day 39).

The idea of authority implied by this personalistic point of view has nothing to do with the idea of office. The idea of office stresses the authority of the office-bearer even as it sets limits on that authority. We are dealing here with the distinction between might or power and official authority. Power goes as far as it can. At a given moment a government may have the power to curtail and suppress all the freedom of both persons and groups. Such power may even receive approval and legal permission. But that does not mean that the exercise of this power is a proper exercise of authority. It is conceivable that a group of persons so governed might even desire this excessive use of power. Such a group might wish the government to concern itself with every imaginable relationship of human life, and that the various spheres might even welcome governmental interference. But this in no way means that interference belongs to the nature of the office.

The office carries within it a certain boundary or limit and it limits the other offices concurrent with it. It is, in a way, a system of mutual checks and balances. Yet it is not up to "ecclesiastical authorities" whether a civil government takes command over the life of the church. Sometimes a government has the power to execute all its commands, be it in accordance with or contrary to the law of the land. Conversely, an indulgent government tolerates a church's, or class's, or movement's meddling in the affairs of civil government. But none of this means that such transgressions of boundaries are justified.

Governmental office exists alongside of ecclesiastical office, and neither has the right to interfere with the other. One office may never usurp the place of another, or infringe upon the terrain of another, unless, of course, some office has degenerated so far that it no longer possesses the right to function. But the point here is that the one office limits and bounds the other, a fact often lost sight of.

Proceeding from the idea of the nation or people (*het volk*) as a unity of blood and soil, there comes an idea something like the idea of office, but maintaining that government is the guide of the nation, exercising all authority over the life of the people. But this violates the special rights of the church, the family, the workplace, and various other spheres of social life. Under such circumstances the church, for example, is silenced if it teaches things in accord with the Word of God which conflict with the directives of the government. The idea of office is then trampled under foot.

Similarly, there are some who ascribe all authority in society to the church. They identify the spiritual with the church and set the spiritual above natural things; therefore, they maintain that the state has only relative independence because it exercises its authority by the grace of the church. In this case, too, the limits implied in the idea of office are contravened.

Indeed, the notion of the limits set on authority is essential to the idea of office. If all authority belongs ultimately to the mandate bound by God to the office, then there can never be a transgression of the limits of the office that is not at the same time opposed to the ordinances of God.

Office and Authority

But what if the acts of the office-bearer cannot be justified; what if they clash with the law of God, as understood by those who are supposed to subject themselves to that authority? This question cannot be avoided.

To be sure, unjustified actions or demands can make it impossible for a Christian to obey. If something is required that would transgress God's command, the Christian must obey God rather than men. Solutions are obvious when one is commanded to deny the name of the Lord, or to abandon work in God's kingdom, or to harm that work.

But the real issue goes much farther, having to do with the whole world of justice and truth, of duty and benevolence, of official task in the world of humanity. For example, we think of the father who must remain head of his family even when something else would usurp his authority, or of those who labor in the scientific disciplines, who must continue to teach the truth at all costs. Indeed, we think of all responsible work upon which no alien principle may intrude.

However, authority cannot be disobeyed just because of an unfair injury or illegitimate demand when that injury or demand does not drive the subordinate to unlawful action. Nor does the principle of lawful disobedience apply when an office-bearer requires an action in an area which falls within the jurisdiction of his office, even if the subject might regard the required action as illegitimate.

For example, in the sphere of the state we have the much debated question of refusing to participate in war and military service. We affirm that there can be just wars, even though they have become more and more rare in a modern world preoccupied with materialism and egoism. We also acknowledge for the individual citizen it is well nigh impossible to judge whether a war in which his government is involved is just or not. Some people believe that when it *is* possible for a citizen to judge a certain war unjust, he should then refuse military service. They often add that under such circumstances he should be willing to accept the consequences of his refusal, being willing even to sacrifice his life for a principle.

But we see here a mistaken way of thinking. The idea of office has not been kept in mind. As long as a subject respects those who govern him as bearers of an office, he may not refuse to obey demands which the governing authorities place upon him in their capacity as office-bearers. Whether he is able or not to judge for himself the justifiability of the action is irrelevant. His obedience is not dependent on his judgment. If the subject thinks he can document injustice, then he must do all in his power to make the government aware of it. But he must accept the government's official order if he cannot dispute the legality of the office itself.

Naturally we, as others, respect conscience. But we judge that a person in doubt should conform his conscience to the directives of Scripture, which teaches us the idea of office. For example, the soldier fighting in war is not acting on his own responsibility, but upon that of his government, which in virtue of its office and its execution has the right to demand obedience and military service.

Thus, in our view, man may not oppose the office that God has instituted, asserting his own will to disobey. And this applies not only in the sphere of the state. The question of military service and conscientious objection is a good example of the general principle under discussion. Another example is the situation of a judge in his court. He is himself the office-bearer, responsible for the exercise of his office, but he may not exercise it purely *according to his own convictions*. The judge is bound to the law and will of legislators.

In the case of a judge who must pronounce penalty on a murderer, it might be that he himself believes that the murderer deserves the death penalty. Yet the judge must impose a penalty according to the law of the land, even if the law of the land does not allow the judge to punish according to what he believes are Scriptural principles of justice.

Another illustration may deepen our insight. According to the laws of some lands, fathers who do not send their children to school must be penalized. Here, the judge must impose the penalty upon the transgressor, even if he believes that a father need give account only to God for the manner in which he has his children educated. The judge must pronounce judgment according to the law of the land; official obedience determines his actions in office.

Dismissal from Office

Sometimes a government does make a demand beyond its right, or one that would make the subject guilty of transgressing the law of God. Such are examples of those who bear office but have lapsed from their office. We should discuss cases of lapse from office at this point.

As we have said, we believe that disobedience to legitimately appointed office-bearers is unjustified. As long as subjects must acknowledge that the government is endowed with authority and as long as its office-bearers act in accordance with their office subjects are bound to obey ruling authorities.

Now, an office-bearer can be declared lapsed. However, the act of so declaring may *never* be an act of one or more persons, but must be itself an official act. Only the power of office may effect expulsion from an office.

To illustrate such a situation, we note first the office of father and mother. Our laws recognize that a government (in this case a judge) may declare a father or mother as lapsed from the exercise of his or her office and thus as divested of parental authority. The law permits this kind of governmental action only under two conditions. First, the parent must be guilty of misconduct in his or her office and must be judged a person unqualified for it. Second, the parent must have neglected and dishonored the office so badly that he or she can be judged to have in effect abandoned or rejected the office.

We draw a second illustration of our point from ecclesiastical life. After confession of faith, members added to the church are entitled to all its privileges and are obligated to all its duties; this is part of entering into the office of believer. The confessing member can be expected to participate in the government and direction of the church; in his official capacity of believer, he occupies a station in the midst of the congregation.

Someone else may sincerely believe that the new member's confession of faith is ingenuine. This sceptical fellow believer can exhort and encourage the new member to seriousness and can even go so far as to indicate the inconsistency between his office and his personal conduct. But never may a member, or even an elder or pastor as *person*, openly doubt the new member's belief, much less obstruct him in the exercise of his office.

Such a task may be undertaken only by an office-bearer of the church. Only the consistory has the right and obligation to exhort, rebuke, and finally obstruct delinquent members from their rights in the church. Finally, only those officially appointed to special office in the church have the authority to declare that the delinquent member has in effect lapsed from his office and then to remove him from the office of believer in the congregation.

These two examples illumine the question of resistance to political authority. When have political leaders lapsed from their office? Never may a gathering of unofficial persons, even if they represent 90% of the populace, set itself up over against the government. All resistance to government which does not procede from office is revolutionary. The Reformers of the sixteenth century were making this point when they said that resistance to governmental authority is justified only when the resisters are led by the "lesser authorities." They meant to say that resistance is justified only when certain rulers themselves could justly declare the supreme government lapsed from its office.

Thus, for example, the resistance of the Dutch against Spain was no revolution but a legitimate action taken by office-bearers of the people. William of Orange, sovereign prince of Holland and Zeeland, and the Estates General, a body constituted by the lesser rulers of the provinces, declared that the supreme governor, Philip of Spain, had indeed abused his office and was thus solemnly deposed as Prince of The Netherlands.

We do not mean to suggest that every person who took part in this affair understood these factors. But this principle was followed, perhaps somewhat intuitively, for at that time various influential disciples of Calvin were teaching these things. Moreover, Calvin himself, on the basis of the idea of office, dissuaded multitudes of oppressed Christians from armed resistance, though he gave his moral support to men of nobility and position when *they* desired to raise the sword against the tyranny of King Francis of France. Furthermore, it was not for practical reasons that Calvin did so—that is, believing that under experienced leadership the rebels might better succeed.

Rather, he urged these courses of action on grounds of principle. He urged what he did because he believed that it was only in this way that resistance and disobedience could be justified.

On the other hand, the French Revolution was truly a revolution, that is, unjustified resistance. It was unjustified not because there were no serious grievances (there were) but because the people, the masses, began the revolution. To such action the people are never called; to such responsibility only office-bearers are called.

We believe that resistance to government can never be grounded in even the noblest purposes or programs of action. Rather, resistance can only be rightly grounded in the official right which leaders of uprisings may possess by virtue of their office, and then only when the ruling government has been judged to have lapsed from office.

We emphasize these matters not out of fear of revolution, but because the zeal with which many people plead for respect for governmental authority seems to be based on spiritual kinship with those in power. We wonder whether the same zeal would remain if leaders of a wholly different political persuasion held power.

Office and the Family

In discussing the family, we turn first to the office of father and mother. This office has existed concretely since the birth of Cain, and at that early time, all other offices and authorities were included in it. Therefore, it is the broadest office; moreover, it is the office most independent of change. Finally, it is obviously an office which exists because of God's creation ordinances.

It may not be entirely correct to say that the state was instituted because of sin; however, we can hardly conceive of its functioning in a world without sin. The same can be said of various other offices. Even the special offices in the church are surely tailored to fit the demands of a sinful world. In a world in which all of God's people would be perfect prophets, priests, and kings, there would be very little place for special offices.

But the office of parent is undoubtedly inseparable from the created, temporal order itself. In the reproduction of humanity, the parental office is transmitted from one human being to another. (We have noted, however, that family is an *institution* of God in which the bearing of children does not automatically imply the right to exercise authority.)

The family's intimate relationship to the order of creation underscores the great importance of this institution and its offices. Our society flows forth from the family. The family is the nucleus of the human race; in it all the ligaments of life are supported; upon it, the flourishing and wellbeing of all relationships depend.

It is crucial for the proper functioning of all the offices that the office of family be properly understood and respected. Since the children of God are the salt of the earth, and we can hardly overestimate their influence, it is crucial not only for the family, but also for human society as a whole that covenant children properly understand the office of father and mother.

The Heidelberg Catechism (Lord's Day 39) says clearly that it pleases God to rule us by the hands of our parents and by all those who are in authority over us. We are thus to obey them, to love and honor them, and to have patience with their weaknesses and shortcomings. We are not asked to be sympathetic to and tolerant of their sins, but to realize that these shortcomings do not cancel the fact that our parents have received an office from God. Their failures do not diminish our calling to respect their office obediently even if we should have to lose much of our natural love and respect for them *as persons*.

The root evil which undermines authority in many other spheres of life is the loss of respect and reverence for the office of father and mother. This grave sin, the diminishment of reverence for the parental office, is not the result of new methods of pedagogy or different relationships that have emerged between parents and their children. We may even be glad that parents and children are freer toward one another and live more intimately together today than in former generations. Now children may participate in family discussions. They are believed to have the right to be reasonably informed about things that once were withheld from them until they had become informed by sources other than their parents.

It is good, then, that we know more about the child's psyche. Yet along with this increased concern for the child's psyche there has emerged an insistence on the child's freedom and independence, for the so called "rights" of the child. Many recommend that the child be left to develop undisturbed by authority figures as much as possible. Two mistaken tendencies surface here. The first is that the child is in himself not so prone to evil, and the second is the diminishment of official authority. Even many Christians believe that because of their limited knowledge of psychology, parents should be the last persons involved with the nurture of children. Many desire to transfer their responsibility to instructors, or "pedagogues," who are actually assistants to the self-nurturing of the child rather than his or her authoritative guide or leader. Children so reared are likely to be easily swayed by slogans that push for emancipation from all authority.

We ought not to deceive ourselves. The spiritual movements and principles operative are like pollution in the atmosphere which penetrates into our lives unnoticed and undesired, filling our homes and clinging to our thoughts. Such pollution must be recognized and banned from our lives.

As the official authority of parents has been undermined in our society, so has come a general weakening of authority. In those circles where people plead for reverence for the authority of the state, there is also a plea that children be obedient to their parents. This spiritual infection is spreading too, and should be a cause for joy, especially among Christians who are concerned for the wellbeing of all of their neighbors.

However, we should be cautious. Two people may say the same thing but mean something quite different. Those who advocate strong parental authority under the tutelage and control of the state often do so in order to inject new life into the state itself. Then the idea of office is not brought to bear. The Christian, on the other hand, acknowledges the authority of parents on the ground of the divine ordinance. It becomes a child to show reverence and obedience to his father and mother because it pleases God to rule him by their hand.

It is the duty of parents to maintain this authority and to give it force. This means that the parent ought to assert the weight of his office, not of his person. A father and mother may well acknowledge their shortcomings and mistakes to a maturing child. Parents can and should tell their children confidently that they themselves are in principle no greater or wiser than their children are. They can also on occasion say, I am much older and more experienced than you and therefore in this matter I know best. But in any case the child should not be told that the reason for his respect and obedience rests in the ostensibly greater capacities or qualities of his father or mother. For then it would be difficult to understand why this special relationship persists even when the child surpasses his parents in knowledge and skill.

It is necessary that parents make it clear that they have been endowed with the authority of the Lord and that therefore it is according to God's plan that the child is subordinate to them, whether or not they are "wiser."

Where parental authority is not maintained, the fault often lies as much with parents as with the children. No sense of inferiority, no consciousness of personal weakness, and no persuasion of one's limitations may lead parents to abandon the office, for it is an office laid upon parents by the Lord.

Chapter 4

Office in the Church

As we take up a discussion of the office the believer holds in the church, we shall touch upon those matters which, in our view, are most neglected. The first matter concerns distinctions among the various offices. Our church offices still seem to be ordered hierarchically. Often most respect is accorded the pastor; next in rank comes the elder; and finally there is the deacon.

Some of this is, of course, understandable. The pastor does indeed devote his entire life to ecclesiastical affairs, having been qualified for the office by long and careful preparation. By contrast, in the minds of members of the congregation and even in the deacon's mind there is the assumption that he does not deal with "spiritual things" because his role involves the financial management of the church.

But even though it is understandable that even consistories think this way, yet this is a serious error which reflects a misunderstanding of office. The offices are indeed distinct, having different natures. But they are not to be arranged hierarchically. In fact it is their differentiation which precludes a hierarchical principle. For example, a deacon who truly understands his office may have the task of admonishing or rebuking an elder or preacher who does not fulfill his responsibility toward a needy person in the church. Similarly, elders are to supervise the doctrine and conduct of the pastor.

The offices, then, are ordered according to the task which is assigned to each office-bearer. Each must limit himself to the sphere of his own office, speaking and acting therein with the authority that has been entrusted to him.

Moreover, the congregation errs when members would rather see the pastor than an elder at their door. When an elder comes in his official capacity, he comes not merely as a brother but as a shepherd appointed to the office by Christ and equipped with a mandate.

Similarly, the congregation errs when it regards the deacon as an advocate for the poor who collects funds for his wards. His office is often lost sight of; in fact, his requests often need the endorsement of the preacher or an occasional admonition from an elder before they are heeded. This should not be so.

When a deacon appeals to the congregation with an admonition to give, he does so *in his office*. Christ thus speaks through him to the congregation, working powerfully and directly through the diaconal function. The diaconate is not a subordinate office. The subordination of offices to one another is a remnant of a Catholic hierarchical system.

The view of our confessions and of the Church Order that no church shall rule over another, nor a pastor over another pastor, nor an elder over his brothers in office must also be applied here and extended to the practice of life. No one office shall lord it over another, nor even be regarded as a higher office. Rather, the relation of the three offices as we know them is one of *cooperation*, in the strictest sense of the word. Leadership in this cooperation shall be by the office most directly involved in any given specific matter. Moreover, in cooperation, the offices together form the council of a church, which, as a whole, acts officially and makes decisions, regardless of which office the individual members represent. The idea of office in the church of Christ must be firmly maintained and not harmed by a ranking of the offices or by a blurring of the distinctions between them. Of course, we also want to acknowledge that in special cases one office-bearer can substitute for another as a *help*, but this principle does not obscure the distinction between offices.

Service and Administration

We would like to comment here on the general nature of the ecclesiastical office. It is often designated as an office of *service*, with reference made to the words of Christ: "He that among you would be the greatest, let him be as one who serves." But this might induce misunderstanding. For Christ was not speaking to a congregation about the special offices of the church; He was speaking to His disciples concerning their communal life *in general*. "Having the character of service" is not a special mark of the ecclesiastical office, but of all offices and all Christian living.

All office is a matter of service; office means that someone does not rule by virtue of his own authority but that he has authority and the right to exercise an office *in the service of God* and therefore in the service of his fellows according to God's command. Whoever assumes power for his own, rather than for God's sake, loses sight of the essential service character of office. He begins to live as if the community existed for him, a destructive situation for all concerned.

The idea of office excludes this, for office is service of God in a specific work—in God's work. Therefore, it is also service as a work of the fellowship which God is building through His work. The servant character of the church comes into being when the children of God have, in the church, a fellowship wherein they can assume offices of service.

But the king on his throne and the father and mother in the family must also serve. In passing we must remark that this service should never be a service of human individuals on account of their worthiness as human individuals. Any office-bearer who serves humanity without first serving God violates the office.

This is also the case in the church. The preacher is neither the servant of the congregation nor of the consistory. Neither is he in practice a ruler over the congregation. In any such case, he injures his service of Christ, and he dishonors his office.

The characteristic aspect or distinguishing mark of the ecclesiastical office is not "service" (diening) but "administration" (bediening). An illustration will perhaps bring clarity. The civil and parental offices are not offices of administration. To these offices God has committed a task which the office-bearer must fulfill in the light of God's Word. These office-bearers have indeed received directives from Scripture, though not prescriptions in detail. The execution of the details is left to the office-bearer, who may make requirements of various kinds and give orders applicable to countless circumstances—which must be followed by virtue of the principle of obedience to the office. The office-bearer takes full responsibility for his commands and expectations.

But this is not the case in the church. Of course there are present elements of individual initiative and personal responsibility. For example, besides being a congregation of believers, the church is an organization which may be either more "democratically" or more "aristocratically" structured without conflict with Scripture. Reformed churches do not hesitate to grant members a strong voice in church affairs and hence a portion of responsibility in, for example, financial decisions and building programs. Yet this dimension of ruling and decision-making recedes into the background when the special offices in the church are functioning properly.

In this context we reiterate that the offices in the church are of an *administrative* character. That is, the office-bearers are called primarily to *administer* the Word of God and the Rule of Christ to the congregation. Thus, the most precise designation of the preacher is the term "minister" (that is, administrator) of the Word. The minister, in distinction from the elder and deacon, is called to preach the Word in the public assembly of the congregation and elsewhere. Moreover, "ministers of the rule of Christ" would be a good title for an elder and "minister of Christ's mercy" for a deacon.

Since the office-bearer in the church is engaged in this kind of "administration," it is not really the case that he pronounces what the congregation must believe and do, based on Scripture and elaborated by his own best judgment. Rather, office-bearers in the church speak what the Word of God says about the faith and practice of the Christian, urging it as a matter of conscience that the congregation listens to, believes, and accepts the Word of God.

In the final analysis, the congregation is required to obey not because the office-bearer has spoken but because the office-bearer in the church is administering the *Word of God*. It is, then, the principal right of the confessing member to investigate whether what has been proclaimed is indeed true, and eventually to liberate himself from what is not in conformity with the Word of God. Hence, to obey and believe simply because an office-bearer has spoken and so to surrender one's own convictions on account of the office is not in order here. In the church, the Word of God and the confessions based on it are primary. Many things may be deduced from the Word and confession, but none of them can bind the conscience simply because they are forthcoming from the office. The right of conscience is embedded in the congregation of Christ, a fellowship of mature persons.

Of course, this does not mean that every member has the right to withdraw himself from the serious and official instruction which the congregation receives from its minister, elders, and deacons. By no means. While we maintain the fallibility of the servant-office-bearer, hoping to escape a Catholic sort of imperialization, we do not wish, either, to encourage an individualism in which the authority of the office in things pertaining to faith and the Christian life would become of no account. An office-bearer must be more than merely a mouthpiece of the people, to execute what they believe and confess. This would destroy the official character of positions of authority in the church. What we do mean to say is that an office-bearer must always ground what he says and does and requires in Christ and the Word of God. When it is not so grounded then it is not binding, nor can it be considered administration of the office. Unlike civil government, the church may not impose and require what it extracts from the Word, for its task is administration of the Word itself. (Of course, the state may not demand and impose what conflicts with the clear teaching of Scripture.)

In the language of Scripture itself, we would say that no one shall rule over conscience in the church. There shall be no masters or lords in the church. No one shall take authority unto himself. In the church of Christ no office-bearer shall demand that anything be confessed, believed, or done purely because he says so.

The Reformed churches have understood this thoroughly and practice it with all seriousness. In fact, it often happens among us that the word of the preacher, elder, or deacon carries little weight because it cannot be supported by a show of learning and eloquence, or by some other personal ability which supposedly guarantees the authority of the office. On the other hand, glorification of office is also occasionally found in the Reformed churches. Preachers are especially venerated, often because people don't take the time to think for themselves. Often the preacher's word is accorded great authority when it has produced a decision favorable to the questioner and no authority when it is unfavorable. This, too, is a case of hiding behind the office.

Power and Authority

Besides administering the Word, the office-bearer in the church administers Christ's right to rule. No man on earth has as much authority as an office-bearer in the church of the Lord; however, this is something different than power, for authority and power do not coincide.

In general the office-bearer in the church lacks the power to compel anyone to do his will. The means of discipline at his disposal are not means of power. He is actually as powerless as the rest of the sheep of the flock.

However, we might also ask where else on earth anyone ever represents the authority of Christ so directly as in the proclamation of the preacher, the visitation of the elder, and the distribution of offerings of the deacon. For this reason, we wish to warn against undervaluing the offices in the congregation of Christ. They bear only an administrative character, but what is administered is God's Word according to Christ's rule. As such, the offices must be accepted, respected and obeyed. They possess genuine authority, and hence, any attack on the office as it rightly administers God's Word is a grave sin.

An example to illustrate: sometimes it is thought that one need subject oneself to the office only when one agrees with the decision or judgment made by the authorities. Such attitudes often emerge in cases of church discipline. An admonished or censured brother or sister appeals the decision of a consistory to classis, and finally to a synod because he is not satisfied with the pronouncement of lesser bodies, even though it cannot be proved that the admonition and pronouncement of the original consistory was in conflict with God's Word.

Moreover, the appeal is often made again and again at the General Synod. If it is to no avail, some may eventually break with the church of Christ because they are not satisfied with the decision reached.

In such resistance there is an utter lack of sense of office. The brother or sister who is admonished by the consistory because of a mistake in doctrine or life must bow before this admonition, unless it can be made apparent that the office-bearers are themselves sinning against the office or against its administrative character.

In many cases of grievance it should be sufficient to tender a respectful and humble protest, so that no "justice" need be sought by way of appeal to a higher body. We are persuaded that most such instances of appeal are born out of stubbornness rather than out of seeking truth, justice, and the administration of God's Word in greater purity than the consistory has done. Often the one admonished is saying in effect, "I won't take orders from such" or "I won't take this lying down." With this the office is denied and the issue is turned into a squabble between two equal parties.

We do not wish to dispute the right to appeal. Our Church Order recognizes this possibility. But we submit that one must not make use of this right too quickly, lest one become guilty of stubbornness, impenitence, and depreciating the office.

Perhaps we can illustrate by reference to a pronouncement of the General Synod concerning membership in several political parties. We are neither defending or condemning this action; we wish merely to make the following observation. Many members of the Reformed Church who were also members of these parties were in a quandary about what to do. To avoid the brunt of the church's pronouncement, they either tried to ignore it or withdrew themselves from the membership of the church.

Now we do not expect this book to be read by those brothers and sisters. Yet we wish to say for the sake of others that to us only one avenue of action appears open, namely, resignation from the political party. This would not have been easy, by any means. But it was impossible to prove from God's Word that the office was being abused and that it could therefore be regarded as lapsed and of no effect.

We are not arguing for or against synod's decision. Our point is this: if a consistory heeds the synodical advice and confronts a member of the congregation with the requirement to break with the political party in question, the church member should acquiesce simply on account of the office. Moreover, he should examine his own view again to determine whether it was in error or not. But even if he continues to believe that the parties in question need not be rejected as unchristian, he should nonetheless, in obedience to the office, surrender his affiliation with the party and find another way to make his political views known.

It may be that the demand of an ecclesiastical office is seen to violate God's Word. In such circumstances the believer-member may not yield. But the many times when this is not the situation, obedience to the office takes priority over the desire to follow personal insight in things that are not directly determinable according to the Word of God.

Differentiating Between Person and Office

We must make mention of yet another sin against the office, one closely related to what has just been discussed. This sin is to regard the person rather than the office.

Occasionally it occurs that a church member is prepared to discuss a difficult matter with a specific office-bearer, or with two or three whom he knows, but wishes to keep knowledge of the situation inside this small circle.

Now we will grant immediately that some who hold office have little conception of their office and are therefore open to the influence of their wives or neighbors. Sometimes it is even said that if the consistory member has a right to know, others who can keep silence may also know. But it is not a matter of the right of anyone to know or of anyone's capacity to protect confidentiality. Rather it is a matter of the difference between being an office-bearer and not being one.

This is only one example of a widespread tendency to regard the person instead of the office. When a member has heard the same preacher "too often" he has come to see the person rather than the office. Sometimes this error shows itself in a preference for a certain elder in family visitation or in catechism. We also often find this neglect of the office when the official work of an elder is at issue and members find it difficult to tolerate his personal idiosyncracies. Even the office-bearers themselves do not constantly ask themselves whether they have the official calling to investigate what they investigate and to say what they are saying.

There is a danger in official visitation that the office-bearer may stress his own personal judgment and evaluation and forget to speak or act solely as office-bearer. The consciousness of office fosters great frankness and confidence in speaking and admonishing, even when the elder knows that he himself is guilty of the very same weaknesses that he is rebuking. However, consciousness of office also fosters great humility and moderation because only as an *administrator of the Word of God* may the office-bearer judge and rebuke as well as comfort and uplift. To forget this official character creates confusion.

As a young pastor I often dreaded admonishing and rebuking a highly regarded member because I thought that this particular member had more experience to admonish and comfort than I. I even thought that he might know more about the life of faith, the confession of the church, and the content of Scripture than I. But remembering one's office can offset this feeling. If one is aware of having received a calling from Christ, diffidence may remain, but faulty hesitation will subside and one will be able to speak and admonish fruitfully.

The office encourages modesty. If one is conscious of bearing an office, then one can easily let one's personal investment lapse. There will be no time to worry about what kind of image one cuts because one's first priority will be doing full justice to the official task. Gradually the urge to act on one's own and to protect oneself will disappear.

We must still exercise great wisdom and discretion in choosing persons for office. On the other hand it is not true that a certain catalog of abilities are prerequisite to holding office. Indeed this matter touches the difficult issue of the relationship of office to gifts and talents. Here a certain balance is required.

It is not the case that the gifts always appear when someone is chosen to office. Naturally, choosing someone for an office is only justifiable when at least a modest show of gifts are present. Yet we may not set a standard for gifts that is beyond the demands of Scripture, lest the need for office-bearers in certain congregations cannot be met.

We should trust that by searching and prayer we will choose those who possess the most gifts and meet the requirements of Scripture. By their official labors God will bless and edify the church. Many a time the church has been more built up by the service of a brother who was chosen in faith, though he had very modest gifts, than by the work of a brother of whose many gifts the congregation was persuaded.

Reasons for Declining Office

Occasionally it occurs that a brother declines the office, but, not having been granted release, persists in his unwillingness to accept because he feels himself unqualified. We would judge that this is in general not permissible. It is not for the brother to judge his own gifts. He must believe that the Lord, who has called him, will use for blessing the gifts that he owns, modest though they be.

Other reasons are also sometimes given for declining official work in the church of Christ, but many of them are arbitrary, arising from the mood of the electee. One who is called to an office is called by the Lord. Unless he can prove that his election is in conflict with Scriptural principles, he should accept the call. Reluctant candidates may argue: humans can err; a consistory can misjudge, unaware of all the circumstances in the life of the member it has chosen. How then, some ask, can anyone, amid all these possible ways to err, know that he has been called by God. Must he not finally feel this calling in his own heart and make a decision after self-examination of his own abilities, time, and the circumstances of his life? To this we would say, emphatically NO!

To be sure, there are hindrances which are signs that the Lord Himself does not wish the person in question to assume an office. We think in particular of sickness and physical handicaps. There is also the possibility that a consistory makes a bad appointment, nominating a brother for office whom they could know should not be chosen. Such appointments are against the directives of Scripture and release from the appointment must be granted.

But apart from these things, one must believe that one has been chosen by the congregation and therefore called by Christ. We believe that the procedure of election by the congregation is the way whereby Christ has ordained to call His office-bearers; hence, one must view the choice as an official call and accept it as such.

Before us there are two options: either it is not correct that Christ calls His office-bearers by way of election in the congregation, in which case we must candidly acknowledge that we have no right to install our office-bearers with the formularies we presently use; or ecclesiastical election is the means Christ uses to fill the offices. When the question, "Do you feel called of the Lord?" is asked a person about to be installed as office-bearer, this does not mean, "Do you have the inward feeling that Christ has called you and do you dare on that basis take the office upon yourself?" Rather what is meant is: "Do you believe that the election that takes place in the church is the way by which Christ calls, and has thus also called you?" Again we would emphasize that the call is valid not because the congregation has done something, but because through the congregation Christ has issued the call. The congregation represents the voice of Christ. For this reason too, one may not decline the call, but may only request release from the call on two kinds of grounds.

One kind of "removal" (*ontheffing*) happens when the office-bearer in question moves away from the local congregation.

The second kind of removal has to do with the case of a person already deeply committed to another place. The additional office to which he has been called would constitute an injury to the first or come into conflict with it. Thus, for example, the office of father (including the task of working in his God-given vocation) would have to be given first consideration. Of course, one might give up a large part of one's daily calling and make a great sacrifice in order to undertake office in the church of Christ. Yet one's daily vocation is an office with a special imperative character; it can never be put aside.

For example, a father may be so preoccupied with guiding his family through particular difficult circumstances that he cannot discharge another office as well. The situation must be judged by the consistory, but often the consistory will leave the decision to the brother in question since he alone knows sufficiently his own family situation.

A similar situation arises when someone has an office in the area of science or civil government. Under such circumstances a consistory may concur with the view that these two offices cannot be undertaken simultaneously without bringing injury to one of the two. But in all of these cases there is no violation of the calling from Christ. Rather, we then have an example of two kinds of calling which bring to test which calling must at a particular moment be pursued singlemindedly according to the Lord's will and which must be let go.

What about a preacher who turns down or declines a call? Why may not an elected elder or deacon do the same? The preacher in this case has two calls at the same time, and he can follow only one: either the call of the congregation that he presently serves or that of the congregation to which he has been called. The situation is one office competing with another office of the same kind. Moreover, the consistory affected by the call grants release from the preacher's present station when it appears that the preacher must follow the lead of the call from the outside. Moreover, if the preacher thinks he must decline the call, his present consistory will view the calling in his present congregation as still binding, and that he is justified in declining the other call. However, if the consistory thinks that the pastor should accept the call to another congregation, then the consistory must say whether it judged this to be best for its own congregation or for the sake of the other. The Church Order is clear that a minister should not leave his congregation without the consent of the consistory. Thus, if the consistory urges the pastor to stay, it must give its reasons.

In the case of the calling consistory, it is customary that there be an acquiescence to the decline of the call, though effort should be made to turn that acquiescence into a consensus, since the decline will have ostensibly been made because of dedication to office.

To decline without sufficient reason is thus not only extremely discourteous but is a disregard of the official calling.

From this it follows that it is unhealthy and unwise even to issue a call when the pastor in question is actually persuaded in his heart that he will not be able to accept. Similarly, candidates for the ministry shall not be able to decline a call unless it can be demonstrated that the call occurred in conflict with Scripture and the Church Order. Naturally the candidate may request an exemption in case he believes that he has shortcomings that would make him incapable of working in the calling congregation. He is also justified to consider additional calls within the time boundaries of the first call.

A few brief comments are still in order about assistants to the pastor. An assistant is normally not called to an office. Hence, he does not have the duty to accept a call if he has reservations, at least not the duty that issues from the idea of office. Certain damage is done to the idea of office when the congregation thinks that the work of the assistant or candidate does not differ in nature and character from the labor of the minister of the Word, who has been called and officially installed. Then the members of the congregation may realize, to their discomfort, that the assistant may not administer the sacraments.

Now, assistants are helpful; however his words are not to be viewed by the congregation as administration of the Word through the mandate of Christ, even though the person in question may feel called to the proclamation of the Gospel in the church of Christ. It should be remembered that neither catechizing nor visitation of the sick nor family visitation is a matter of special office. In sum, we should not blur the principial difference between words of evangelism and the official administration of the Word in an office. Moreover, we should not needlessly neglect the establishment of an office in all of its aspects where this is at all possible.

Chapter 5

Office of the Believer

We must also discuss the office of the individual believer. The idea is expressed in the 28th Article of the Belgic Confession as follows: "We believe . . . that all men are *in duty* bound to join and unite themselves with (the holy congregation) . . . And that this may be more effectually observed, it is the duty (office) of all believers, according to the Word of God, to separate themselves from all those who do not belong to the Church and to join themselves to this congregation, wheresoever God has established it . . . ."

With this quotation we touch upon a very important question concerning the idea of office. During the *Doleantie* (a movement in 1886 during which *Grievances* were brought against the Dutch Reformed Church of The Netherlands) the office of believer was given honor and clearly brought to the foreground. It was affirmed that special office-bearers in the church and members of the church are co-responsible for the church's affairs. Moreover, believers are to be more than passive in their concurrence with what happens.

The believer has a task in the church of God, as is recognized when the approval of the congregation is sought in the nomination and calling of office-bearers, in granting and receiving of church membership, and in the processes of censure. There are matters that do not touch the office of believer, such as the financial and organizational aspect of congregational life. But it is the office of the believer by silent acquiescence to cooperate in the installation of persons into the special offices, to recognize the full membership of those who were formerly minors, to declare that those are outside of Christ who have been excommunicated, to accept those who present proper membership papers from other churches, and so forth. If a believer does not feel able, by virtue of his office, to acquiesce in the action, then he must make known his objection. The believer should then cooperate in the rectification of the relation, cooperating with a view to a well-deliberated decision and toward the maintenance of properly functioning church offices.

The involvement of the congregation in the actions of the consistory can, of course, extend much farther than acquiescence. Some congregations recommend, by vote, some brothers to stand for election, and then elect some of that group.

This action is not a necessary complement to the office of believers; if it were, it would be impermissible to exclude women from election of special office-bearers. They partake of the office of believer as well as men and thus they are equally invited to participate in the approbation of actions taken by the special office-bearers.

This real, proper work of approbation always continues and never stands still. It belongs to the office of believer, and is a very important element in the life of the church of Christ. It must be well understood and highly regarded both by the special office-bearers and by the members of the congregation. It should never be viewed as a mere formality, and certainly never as a silent relinquishing of responsibility.

By approbation, members of a congregation give support to the consistory, approving its action. This does not entail a notion of popular sovereignty, a sort of unspoken majority vote. Rather, the meaning of approbation is that by supporting the consistory, the congregation shares in the responsibility.

When believers by their silence tacitly approve calls or appointments and then later question or complain about them, they have misused their office. The congregation should be more conscious than it is that it is by virtue of their office that they give approbation. There is much responsibility here.

Treatment of Each Other

When we consider the office of all believers, we must consider our relationships to one another. Are we in our treatment of one another to proceed from the objective or the subjective; from the covenant or from the personal life of faith; from the idea of office or from the person.

We have seen that the idea of office gives us a correct balance in many areas of life; a proper balance between an external relationship which may be superficial and status quo and inner values based on personal standards of judgment. In connection with the idea of covenant and self-examination, we face the same task of balancing. When wondering who is to be regarded as a Christian and child of God, we can proceed from the external givens: that one has received baptism and belongs to a definite church. In this case one takes the covenant in its broadest sense.

On the other hand, we might proceed from the conviction that things are not as they seem. Then both our evaluation of covenant members and our evaluation of ourselves before God continually remain uncertain—at least until it becomes clear that in someone a work of God has been wrought.

Now as long as the church waits for Christ's return, there will be conflict between these two kinds of evaluation. We know from Scripture that only those will be saved whom God through His sovereign grace has elected, and will in time lead to faith in Christ, perhaps even in the last moments of life. All others are rejected, in spite of their saying "Lord, Lord." The Lord has said that except a man be born again by water and the Spirit, he cannot see the Kingdom of God. This regeneration by the Spirit is as hidden as the wind: you hear it, but you do not know whence it comes and whither it goes; so is everyone born of the Spirit. Our partial knowledge of these things will always remain partial.

Similar questions can be asked about the truths of the covenant and the sacraments. At the baptism of adults and of children alike, the Lord says that He establishes His covenant with them, that He wills to wash them with His blood, and that He wills to make them partakers of Christ and all His benefits.

Christians also affirm, Scripturally, that the entire multitude of church members can be addressed as sanctified and beloved, as brothers and sisters, as those who are born again, not out of perishable but imperishable seed. They may say that they all belong to the household of God, and that the rich benefits of the Lord are given to the whole congregation, who are all together warned against apostasy.

Concerning this last matter, two themes appear in Scripture. On the one hand there is the clear promise that He who has begun a good work in us will complete it right up to the day of Christ. On the other, there is the clear and urgent warning that none should fail to obtain the grace of God and that no one who has tasted the heavenly gifts should withdraw unto his own destruction and thus crucify the Son of God afresh.

Here one can err in one of two directions. One can assume that election and regeneration are the major truths taught in Scripture, relativizing all others. Or one can follow the other train of thought, subordinating the truths of election and rebirth to the covenant and the confession. One then proceeds with the practical attitude that a person born and living in the covenant and in the circle of confessors must be regarded as belonging to the elect, leaving the final questions for eternity.

Some people have tried to escape this difference by speaking of an internal and external covenant. But this only shifts the difficulty; it does not resolve it. The external covenant would mean very little, and the internal covenant would still be a mystery.

Office and Calling

We must begin elsewhere—with the notion of believer as office-bearer. This idea is of great importance; for office means "being called by God, or appointed and clothed with dignity." Office means being justly appointed to a certain station in life. A believer is then established as a believer by something more substantial than an inner disposition, an attitude, or even the influence of the Holy Spirit. In the context of office, we must speak of more than faith, of the marks of true faith, and about doubt and assurance.

These subjects are indeed very important, but they bring on much confusion when the *office* of believer is overlooked. The problem we are addressing is subjectivistic onesidedness in the realm of faith, such as is associated with Anabaptism, mysticism, and Methodism. Even in our circles people often speak of faith as a state, a deed, an inner conviction, an attitude of life of the individual person. And since no person can ever look into another's heart, it can never be perfectly clear that another person is truly a believer. Other questions follow: Does the person in question really have a self-evident spiritual life? Does he appear before others and in public as an undeniably persuaded believer? Does he speak forth and "testify" of the hope that is in him?

We should emphasize once more that we too are persuaded that faith must be an inner conviction, a being incorporated into Christ, a union with the Savior of sinners, and thereby with the Triune God. True faith is not only a sure knowledge whereby we hold as truth all that God has revealed to us in His Word, but also a firm confidence which the Holy Spirit works in our hearts that to us the grace of Christ is freely given. This faith *will* become evident; if it is true faith, it will be expressed. Whoever does not believe with his heart and confess with his mouth, be it only in his last moments and in the inner chamber, is no child of God and will be lost because he has not believed in the Son of

God, however blameless his external life may have been.

But there is more. First, a man's inner conversion is not an achievement; believers do not constitute an "elite" class of humanity. On the contrary, faith as a condition of the heart is a gift and creation of God the Holy Spirit, even though man is active and responsible in his believing.

Second, God does not follow the procedure of making man a believer and working faith in his life by His Word and Spirit without respect for the wide varieties of human nature. God does not give us a fixed standard by which we can determine in others and in ourselves whether faith is present and flourishing.

We have all noticed how many types of human character there are, for example: sanguine, choleric, phlegmatic, and melancholic. We also know that no person belongs perfectly to any one group.

Now there is something of this in the life of faith also. Because life is complicated, one cannot always distinguish the believer from the unbeliever. Even when dealing with a believing person, one's judgment of his or her commitment often proves mistaken. We can even feel despair about ourselves, for we can point to as many signs of unbelief in ourselves as to expressions of a heart turned to God in love.

We do not wish to downplay the value of self-examination, but wish to stress something else as well. We wish to emphasize that such self scrutiny and such examination of others may never become a judgment of the salvation of oneself or another. Even when one says today that one believes and tomorrow that one does not, one can take comfort from the thought that the work of the Holy Spirit cannot perish.

But in all of this, we need another standard by which to judge whether anyone is in the faith or not. *And God has given us that in the office of believer*. But even this may be misunderstood. Many a sect calls the "truly born again" to band together and to constitute a special body. In this way, they also press the mark of unbelief on many who are marked differently by God. When we do such things, we have appointed ourselves judges where the judgment of God alone can be accepted and honored.

The standard which matters is God's. God appoints men to be believers. He nominates them to the office of believer, promises them gifts, gives them responsibilities, and thus establishes a standard to which we can orient ourselves, and by which we can judge. Believers are those who live under the discipline of the Word and Spirit, and thus under the discipline of the office.

The Apostle Paul knew very well that in the churches to which he wrote the unfaithful were mingled in with the true children of God. There was chaff among the grain. Paul wrote to the congregation of Corinth that he was determined to surrender to satan the fornicator who had his father's wife that his spirit might be saved in the day of the Lord (I Corinthians 5). It is also true that this did not mean the end of the threat. In the same chapter Paul wrote further of the obligation of the congregation to judge and to remove the evil one from their midst.

In the letter to Timothy, Paul no longer speaks of a threat, but he assigns Timothy to fight the good fight and to preserve the faith, "which some have rejected and suffered shipwreck in regard to their faith; among whom are Hymenaeus and Alexander, whom I delivered over to satan, so that they may be taught not to blaspheme" (I Timothy 1:20). Thus, even in his circle of co-workers Paul had experienced disappointment. To the Colossians he transmitted the greetings of Demas, evidently one of his co-workers, designating him as such in the letter to Philemon. And yet in II Timothy 4:10, he complained that "Demas has forsaken me, having come to love the present world."

Now what is Paul's response? Knowing the chaff among the grain, does he leave the church in order to establish a sect of pure and holy people? This option never enters his mind! Paul does not hesitate to continue calling the church "brothers," "congregation of God," "sanctified ones in Christ," "those called to be saints," and the "flock of God."

At the same time, Paul speaks of falling from the faith, of rejecting the faith, and of the children of the kingdom who are cast out. Thus, while he describes the body in terms of its true members, he does not include within it both those who have the right to the title of believers and others who do not.

What are we driving at with all this? Are we accepting the idea that saints can fall away, thus overthrowing one of the articles of the Reformed confessions? And are we in conflict with the teaching of Paul when we maintain the impossibility of such a falling away?

Hopefully we are all convinced that no one can snatch from the hand of Christ those whom the Father has given Him. And we believe that there is the term or title "believer" which refers to a position, or office, and to a responsibility or task. Our criterion of evaluation is that God has placed the person in that office and that we therefore have to respect him as a believer fully and without hesitation until he himself by word and deed proves himself unworthy of the office, having scornfully rejected it and having thus lapsed from the office.

All of the members of Christ's church hold this office when, under the discipline and preaching of the Word, they present themselves as believers. By virtue of birth, baptism, and confession of faith they belong to the congregation of believers, having received and accepted all of the rights and duties thereunto apertaining.

With these believers we may count the children who by virtue of baptism are incorporated into the Lord's church. Of course, we do so only in a certain sense, for these children are actually only candidates for office in so far as they can not perform the duties required. We do not wish to exclude them because even in their being called to office there is an official position that we may not neglect. However, we should first talk about the *office* of adult believer.

We have referred to this station and calling as an office because in it all the marks of office are present. There is first of all the appointment, most obvious in baptism whereby the child is received into the church of Christ. Every believer comes to his station by divine ordination.

Adult believers have also accepted the office in an act of public profession of faith, or else this basic appointment and acceptance has come to expression in the act of adult baptism. Whether or not time elapses between the appointment and the response of acceptance does not bear on the question of whether or not a person occupies the office of believer. To be a covenant child is to hold an office, the office of having been made holy in Christ, the office of being reckoned as one of Christ's and thus as being separated from the children of the world. The child has been placed in a position that belongs with the office. The treasures and gifts of Christ are presented to him and placed in his hands for him to appropriate as his own. He is placed in the congregation of Christ, the working-sphere of the Holy Spirit, so that he experiences the Spirit in the sense of Hebrews 6:4. He is marked and designated as one of those who belong to Christ. He bears Christ's mark and insignia (Belgic Confession, 34). He has the duty and right to lay claim to all the promises of God. He need not ask anxiously whether he is elect or reborn, but must proceed from the covenant and from his official appointment. On that ground he may ban all doubt and unbelief, as he meekly and humbly takes to himself the grace of God in Christ as given to him.

But naturally it is possible to hold an office legally and yet to plunder it or to lack the gifts and talents needed to discharge it. In just that way, it is possible to trample underfoot the office of believer. Sometimes one becomes aware of having done this only later, having as a child been placed in the office and having been confirmed therein by holy baptism.

No human may meddle with this appointment. The person himself is not free to be released of it by simply declining. One cannot decline an office granted by the King of kings and Lord of lords; one can only reject it in sinful rebellion.

All of the characteristic marks of office apply also to the office of believer. It may happen that one esteems the believer himself highly because he lives out of his faith. But such is his *calling*, even though one may not perceive that the gifts and virtues displayed in his exercise of an office relate to the office.

The second characteristic of the office of believer is that it can be lost, though only in a divinely ordered manner. Even a father and mother can lose their office, though they can never lose their existence as source of the life of their children.

Discipline and Office

I wish to speak here about the true and faithful discipline that must be exercised over every office, including the office of believer. Surely the office carries with it the demand to be assumed worthily and according to God's regulation. The office-bearer must believe and conduct himself as a believer in word and deed. In short there should be no conflict between the office and the praxis of the bearer. Yet when there is an inconsistency, the very sanctity of the position should restrain everyone from pronouncing hasty judgment on the Lord's anointed. On the other hand, that same sanctity of office means that any misconduct which disgraces the office will be taken very seriously.

It is often said that those who belong to the covenant (in the external sense) must be acknowledged and regarded as such because we do not know otherwise and because we cannot look into the heart. The real reason that we must treat one another as covenant members goes further: otherwise we might risk depreciating one of the true children of God, causing him to stumble. Just as we are to acknowledge everyone in office, regardless of mistakes and shortcomings, so too we are to acknowledge covenant members in their office until the time that they are declared lapsed from the office.

If anyone refuses to acknowledge as a covenant member one who later proves to be a covenant breaker, he has still dishonored an office granted by God. Moreover, if we accept all apparent covenant members as those who are in office, and then someone departs from the fellowship, it is he who has broken covenant. We will have kept the covenant in our acknowledgment of him who broke it, until that breach became visible.

Just as in the world, other kinds of office are normally bestowed through orders established by God and can be so withdrawn, so in the church of Christ, investiture takes place through the consistory, through those who have been appointed for the leading and organizing of the congregation as church of Christ. This consistory causes the baptism of children to be administered. It must abstain from all arbitrariness, keeping itself strictly to the mandate of the Lord of the church. No one may encroach upon this, neither by rash baptism of those who do not belong to the church, nor by a denial of baptism to those in whom there are indications of God's presence. The Word of God also lays the grounds for baptizing the children of believing parents.

It is also the task of the consistory to give supervision and guidance for public profession of faith as believers advance from minority to majority in their office-bearing, from baptismal membership to participation in the Lord's Supper. Again all arbitrariness is to be avoided. The Lord has indicated that the only standard is confession and conduct, nothing more and nothing less.

According to its high calling and tremendous responsibility, the consistory must also guard the sacredness of the office on the basis of God's Word and must depose from the office when and where necessary. This deposition becomes necessary when an erstwhile believer refuses to make a confession of faith and live accordingly.

Of course, this is at times difficult. For example, we have a deep regard for the Confessions and for the Reformed conception of life. Now it may happen that someone among us departs somewhat from the Reformed Confessions, or that his or her conduct conflicts with the Reformed view of life, causing disturbance and disharmony.

In such cases members of the congregation may feel like saying that this person is a Christian, but not Reformed. We have no place for him; let him depart or else we will have to come down on him. Of course there are churches besides the Reformed Church where the member might fit in better. However, we must at all costs maintain the office of believer of this member, the office in his own congregation, however difficult it might be and however much exhortation is necessary.

If there is actually a continuing transgression of the commands of God, be it in doctrine or life, then surely the bearer of the special office must deny the sinner first the exercise of the general office, and then, if necessary, also the possession of it. But until such a time everyone shall also follow the example of David, who still honored Saul in his office when the Lord had rejected him, the sentence having not yet been executed. In addition all fellow-believers must guard against Samuel's sin of desiring, out of personal love, to maintain one whom the Lord has deposed. "One office in judgment over another" should be the watchword here.

From this several consequences flow. First, as we noted earlier, a lapse from office can only be pronounced by an office. This process takes place when censure has advanced to the point where in Christ's name the office declares that this person must be accounted a publican and sinner. However, as long as this pronouncement has not been made, the person in question is a brother or sister. Of course, the exercise of his office, though not the office itself, may be suspended whenever there is good reason for serious criticism.

Second, official censure applies not only to professing members but also to baptized members, that is, persons who are in the office of believer but who have never taken full responsibility for it. When a consistory judges that the covenant has been broken and that the office has been rejected, then official deposition must follow. The pronouncement must take the form of a cancellation, so that the office is no longer in effect. However, it has been said that baptism can not be undone, and this is undoubtedly true. In fact, the covenant is not even undone for those who continue to persevere in breaking it. Rather, his baptism will forever mark the covenant breaker as one who has disavowed the covenant. For the sake of the breaker, it might be wished that baptism could be undone.

Not everyone who has been baptized remains in office. The covenant and the idea of office demand a confessional church that exercises discipline. Otherwise the covenant is profaned, not only by the individual covenant breaker, but by the "church" which allows itself to become a mixed multitude.

Scripture demands that only believers and their offspring may be installed to the office of covenant membership. If this demand is ignored, the stability of the covenant is lost and all the blessings accruing from it are squandered. However, the effect of the covenant can never be removed; the judgment against covenant breakers now falls on the whole congregation.

In our opinion, not all those baptised in other churches should be considered covenant members. Baptism in a State Church or in the Roman Catholic Church, for example, does not necessarily mean appointment to the office from God. Our "recognition" of the baptism of other churches means nothing other than that we recognize it in retrospect, when someone so baptised actually accepts the office, or when his parents do. In such cases, the formality of baptism had validity and can thus be regarded as legal and not in need of repetition.

To continue to enjoy the covenant and the sharing of the covenant, it is necessary that the church exercise discipline. Discipline must maintain the office by removing from it those who have lapsed, and by forbidding the exercise of its rights to those who by word and deed live in conflict with it. Moreover, the church must be a confessional church, because only with regards to a known confession, and conduct which follows from it, can the office-bearer be known to accept his office.

We might add here that weaknesses and mistakes do not cause the church to lose its character as a disciplinary church; rather it loses this essential character when it shrugs off the duty of discipline and thereby knowingly surrenders this official position.

Concerning preaching, if we see before us merely a congregation of elect and reprobate, then we can omit the preaching of repentance and the call to accept Christ. If we proceed from the idea of belonging either "internally" or "externally" to the covenant, then we need to speak to two separate groups in the congregation. But with the true idea of covenant, both of these alternatives disappear.

The call to faith and repentance must be continued, for faith and repentance are the way in which the acceptance of the office continues to take place, as it must. We must always examine ourselves to determine whether we are genuinely performing our office and keeping the covenant, that is, living in faith and repentance.

However, the believer has no right to question whether God has really placed him in office. He should not doubt that God has given him the gifts of Christ, the call to accept them trustingly, and the warning not to reject them in breach of the covenant. Furthermore, the believer ought not to stop praying for the Holy Spirit to renew his heart and to lead him into all truth.

The idea of office also tells us much about the practice of life in the covenant. God has appointed us and our children, as we have said. When one of our children dies young, without having broken the covenant and faithlessly forsaken the office, we may not doubt the salvation of this child, but must firmly believe that our God will maintain his appointment, which He has confirmed by the sign and seal of baptism.

As our children mature in the ways of the Lord's covenant, we may live in trust. The eyes of father and mother search, with prayer and longing, for signs of the life of faith and devotion. At an age when this piety should be manifest and is not, parents may grieve and pray earnestly for their children's repentance. But when the child is too young to give a clear manifestation of a conscious fear of the Lord, then parents must not be anxious, or look in suspicion at their children, wondering whether they are children of the covenant. One cannot harvest ripe fruit from a freshly planted sapling.

It does happen, too, that a child who comes to piety early goes totally astray in later years; the early piety proved not to have been true faith. It could have been a childlike emotional imitation of what was heard in the child's surroundings—which in a child is far from being hypocritical. Here too the idea of office is helpful. When the children of Jerusalem shouted "Hosanna" to the Son of David, the Lord was gladdened by this, even though these children were imitating adults. Jesus even said that those children had brought real praise to God.

When Samuel gave the beautiful response: "Speak Lord, for your servant hears," he was repeating Eli's words. We would probably doubt Samuel's piety. The Bible even says that Samuel did not as yet know the Lord.

But neither does the Bible expect this of Samuel at this point. Naturally, this first conversation with the Lord was the beginning of Samuel's further standing in service of God, in whose service he indeed had already stood.

Accordingly, when our little children say their prayers at their mother's side, they are keeping the covenant. When at home and at school they learn their texts and recite their Bible verses and reverently listen to prayer, then they are not only being instructed in the keeping of God's covenant, but they are also keeping the covenant themselves. They are indeed executing their office.

Self-examination

We conclude with some remarks about confession of faith.

On the one hand it is often said that profession represents a "good choice" made at a decisive point in life. The young person chooses for the service of God when he or she makes public profession of faith. In this way of viewing the matter the connection with baptism is largely ignored. No great difference appears between this choice and the choice of a young person who comes from an unbelieving home and asks for baptism into the church of Christ.

On the other hand, public profession of faith seems sometimes little more than cordial agreement with the Confession of the Church and the truth of Scripture. Such agreement does not involve personal faith and participation in Christ, and such a confession is not the same as conversion and having received the Spirit. This must then still come, or be added later. Or so some people say.

But this is an impossible point of view. According to the Reformed Confession, Word and sacrament are indivisible. One cannot accept the Word of God and appreciate his Christian nurture and yet refuse or doubt his share in Christ. Either this doubt is completely unjustified or the confession is not true.

Confession of faith is, by definition, an open and official acceptance of the covenant, of the office in which one was placed before birth, and installed in baptism. Confession of faith means accepting this baptism, saying "yes" to the position of office-bearer, and praying that one will remain thus by the grace of Christ. Confession of faith is not a sudden "choice"; it is an oath of fidelity which one must declare—not as the alternative to serving another Lord, but as an alternative to deserting the position of office-bearer for the Lord who has marked him with His seal. Whoever does not declare is marked as a covenant breaker, not as one who has made the wrong "choice" from a neutral position.

Making confession as a mere formality is no worse or better than casually waiting for the right moment. Nor is it better than making no confession at all. The only alternative to making confession of faith under false pretenses or to piously neglecting to do so is to make confession out of a faith prayerfully requested and gratefully accepted from the Lord as a promised gift.

We must scrutinize ourselves carefully concerning our place in the church and in the covenant. The covenant requires that we live continually as believers and children of God. Yet the demand is beyond our abilities to fulfill. Moreover, we are called to be holy, even as God is holy; only perfection completely fulfills the office of believer.

Scripture always reiterates this requirement and therefore also always presses for repentance, both from specific sins and from our sinful attitude in life, which we all share as one in Adam. But at the same time Scripture always assures us that perfection is granted and prepared for those who believe, not as something that transcends their position, but as the only fitting completion and fulfillment of their life and redemption.

Therefore, the great struggle of the children of God on earth is not that they have to suffer oppression and sorrow, but that they have to struggle constantly against sin and always fall short of the promised perfection. Their comfort is that they will attain to this perfection, even if only in the life to come.

This struggle is no small matter. If someone does not feel the actual burden of the struggle, he does not take seriously enough the perfection to which we are called. However, there are also those who grieve over the fact that they have not taken their office seriously enough. They waste their time and energies in the drudgery of probing the question whether they indeed are in office instead of pressing on in confidence, prayer and dedication to the faithful God who has called them.

We should not minimize the seriousness of their struggle; there are brothers and sisters in our churches who are genuinely fearful. But we must press home the fact that Scripture shows that only those who boast of their own accomplishments are in danger of being forsaken. Only those who claim the office on the basis of their own accomplishments are in danger of hell-fire. And, in fact, those who are unsure of their salvation are often preoccupied with the things that they do.

But how far they have wandered from the proper path! There is a great difference between those who are cast out and those who are fearful. Even though the latter acknowledge their sinfulness and unworthiness, they are still imagining that their salvation depends upon themselves.

Both should take seriously the truth that man is not placed in office on account of his attainments. By grace alone, God makes us His children and gives us the place where we may stand, assuring us of the blessings and gifts of grace in Christ. In our struggle to fulfill our office, we can always fall back on the gracious act of God, which is the reason for our being in office.

Therefore we may not squander our energy and courage with drudgery and worry, nor may we neglect the gifts that have been given us. To be sure, members of the covenant are called to continual self-examination. But how often and when must this be done?

Is self-examination one point in the Christian program, among others? Something that can be done too little or too much? Isn't it rather the case that self-examination is always a calling *under specific circumstances and in specific situations*? When the situation does not present itself, then self-examination is not necessary. For example, when the preaching of the Word points to our sins and failures, urging us on to love and faithfulness, then we must examine ourselves. With the congregation we confess that with body and soul both in life and in death we belong to our faithful Savior Jesus Christ, and that this is our only comfort. Self-examination is in order here, for to stand properly before God we must *rejoice* in this only comfort. We must rest and rely on it with all our heart. We must ask ourselves to what degree do we accomplish this and what is our thanks to God for His great salvation?

We might offer another example. During the experience of

war, many of us hated our enemies bitterly and despaired about the future of our families, state and church. Now Scripture says over and over again that those who fear the Lord have nothing to fear, that we must love our enemies, and that our cause is surer and firmer than the rocks and mountains. How is it that our war experiences did not correspond to this description (prescription) in Scripture? We face again the call to repentance, the call to set ourselves more completely at the disposal of God.

Finally, we might give the example of participating in the Lord's Supper. We may go to church and partake of the Lord's Supper faithfully without experiencing much benefit. We are inclined to ascribe this deficiency to the preacher or to the church. We may regard the preaching as barren, lifeless, dull, or not personal enough. We all know the experience.

It doesn't help much to say that it is God's Word that is being preached; the quality of the preaching must indeed be taken into account. Criticism of the preacher may indeed be proper. But it should be done in the preacher's presence or in the presence of those who are able to speak with him or to him about it.

Besides the matter of the quality of preaching, however, there is also room for self-examination and self-criticism. We should ask ourselves whether the cause for our apathy might be lack of interest, lack of prayer, and lack of serious concentration on the proclamation of the Word. Is it not possible that we participate in the church and in the Lord's Supper as a routine, almost on the assumption that blessings will rain down upon us automatically?

The examples we have given show that self-examination is imperative. It is not a continuing condition but a repeated call which we hear when we are confronted with the glories of Christ and our own lack, and our sin presses down upon us.

Self-examination, when it occurs, is always examination about the exercise of our office, about our keeping of the covenant, about our living out of the Word and by the Spirit, about the exercising of our faith. Thus it is continually a criticism of ourselves, but also a source of great joy when we see God's grace come to manifestation in our lives in actual confidence and trust in God.

Sometimes something wholly different is meant by the idea of self-examination, something destructive, namely, continuing to ask: do I stand in the covenant; have I received the office; do the promises of God apply to me; may I partake of the Lord's Supper and appeal to my baptism? Now, this is not self-examination, but an examination of the oaths and promises of God, of the covenant and calling of God. About this we may, of course, inquire, on the condition that we immediately accept our calling in faith. We have no basis to doubt the surety of God's promises and assurances; in fact, such doubting is ungodly. We may only inquire about the promises of God in order to have greater assurance of faith.

Even the term "self-examination" can be misleading—as if it were an examination that one initiates oneself, to see whether one genuinely believes, has real faith, is actually alive within, and is truly converted—without the assurance of which all prayer and singing, all profession of faith and celebration of the Lord's Supper cannot be called true. This self-directed, introspective approach to self-examination is unreal and in conflict with the teachings of God's Word and Spirit. Such self-examination is not living in God's Word but stirring oneself up emotionally. Some may respond that one must observe and take note of the expressions of life and spirit; these will show whether one has been accepted by God's grace. But I object to this for two reasons.

I object first of all because the knowledge that one is adopted by God cannot be based on one's life experience. It rests, instead, in the promises of God, and in the work of Jesus Christ. We can be glad that that is so. For surely if our own experience were the basis of our assurance, that assurance would depend wholly on our own skill in evaluating the meaning of our experience and expressions. Lifelong doubt would ensue, because one could never be sure of one's own diagnosis. In fact, those who practice this kind of self-examination are indeed frequently plagued with lifelong doubts, leading others into doubt with them.

Furthermore, adoption as God's children precedes life itself. God does not adopt persons because there is life in them. Rather He gives them life because He has adopted them to be His children. Scripture asserts that a sinner who does not have the Spirit is dead in sin, and that the natural man does not understand the things of the Spirit of God. So either one of two things is the case: either one is indeed dead, and one's religious life is a sham, or one is alive in the Spirit. If dead, then one can never examine whether one is truly alive. How can a dead man even know that he is dead? Examining, proving, testing; these are all actions, and actions are deeds of the living.

Even nature proves our point. A farmer doesn't examine a plant at its roots, but rejoices in the fruit it bears. Or, again, one knows that one is physically alive when one uses one's arms and legs in working, thinking, and speaking. One feels alive, but never undertakes research to test that life.

I remember with deep emotion a conversation with a sister from one of our Reformed churches. For years she had been preoccupied with a search for her regeneration. She had been told that she would surely recognize it as a momentous experience. It was pointed out to her, by way of illustration, that as mother she surely knew that the birth of a child is not something that passes unnoticed. This depressed her greatly, for surely she had not had a religious experience comparable to childbirth.

Light broke when she discussed these things with a simple and wise elder who picked up her narration with the words, "But as a mother you surely know that childbirth is a complicated happening." The mother nodded, and the elder responded with the question, "Did your baby know this too?" Then this woman saw her sin. In the life of faith she wanted to be the mother, though actually she was a child. She herself wanted to effect control, to trace her rebirth by the Holy Spirit, instead of simply living out of her birth. This simple question of the elder turned the woman's life around.

There is another, healthy kind of "self-examination." It is an investigation seeking the firmness and sureness of God's promises. It is an investigation that is actually taking refuge in and trusting God's promises, an investigation that by faith looks to the firmness of God. This genuine self-examination searches out the deeds of faith, the failures and fruits, the stumblings and the recoveries, the changes and the variations in the life of faith. This is done not to acquire firmness or doubt, but is done to rejoice in God's grace and to repent from sinful wandering. On the basis of the office given to a believer, this true self-examination criticizes and corrects the exercise of that office.

One question still remains. I can imagine that some reader will ask why I spend so much time controverting something that I insist is not valuable or even real. But I am talking about a practical problem.

Suppose that there is someone who has been induced to serious and prayerful self-examination. Soon he will find himself trapped, and without hope of final assurance. Surely, if one probes into oneself for evidence of spiritual life, one can perhaps conclude that there are strong positive signs. But a week from now, when taking another examination, the signs of life may be very weak, so that assurance turns to doubt.

When one does not find enough proof of spiritual life to dare to say that it is well with one's soul, one clings to the hope that those signs may appear. And so one oscillates between doubt and hope. The anxiety induced is not the worst of it; the worst evil is that one has aroused and nourished one's own doubt concerning what God does and gives.

But do we seriously think that by self-examination we can

even renew our own lives? Surely, as biblical Christians of Reformed persuasion, we heartily confess that regeneration is a work of the Holy Spirit. God has spoken to say that He wills to be our God. Is not that the first and final appointment to the office of believer?

Hundreds of believers, weak in faith, are in murky darkness for their entire lives because they do not seek their stability in God's promises but seek it rather in themselves, in self-examination. Of course, they say that they are seeking their assurance in the work of the Spirit. But this is largely self-deception. If they do come through, this is an unmerited and unexpected gift of God's grace, who grants them what they are busily engaged in endangering.

And then there is the other side: all those people who are alienated by this talk of self-examination, and so never achieve real and proper self-examination. They throw the baby out with the bathwater. These are inclined to say to their pastor: "You had better do your task and continue doing it; we are unconverted." It is clear to them that if one's assurance of faith rests in the fruits of self-examination and in daring to count oneself a member of the kingdom, then one is powerless to make himself belong. But all of this is wrongheaded.

God's work through the Word is appointment to the office of believer and a calling to faith and repentance. We live according to the Word, and in this office we have our work and responsibility. In our bearing of office lies our stability.

Chapter 6

The Office of Believer and Ecclesiastical Life

All believers share the general office, and therefore they all have responsibility for building of the body of Christ, caring for the worship service, and so forth, even though the administration of the church is assumed by only a few.

Let me stress then that ecclesiastical life is not a matter that should concern office-bearers only. Indeed, people come to church gladly, participate in sacrificial giving, and are occasionally willing to do this or that for the cause of God. But they are not aware that the life of the church is our collective concern. This is not sufficiently felt. But since we all as believers constitute the church, the church's concerns and well-being belong to us no less than to persons occupying the special offices. Were this truth to root more deeply in our souls, we would be able to discuss more easily the office of believer.

Church Attendance

We all attend worship service on Sunday by virtue of our office as believers. The Psalmist sang, "I was glad when they said to me, 'Let us go up to the house of God.' " Church attendance is, of course, a matter of necessity as well as of desire and joy. Church attendance is according to the command of God, and it also fills a need in us. Whoever does not feel a need to honor God in this way and to hear the proclamation of the gospel of Christ does not attend church properly. Indifference during this most serious event, the meeting of God with His people, is no slight sin. Thus it is fitting that we pray for a heart that longs for the courts of the Lord because it thirsts for the living God.

But none of this conflicts with worship attendance by virtue of the office of believer. We can expand our theme to say that we attend worship out of a genuine need to serve God and fulfill the office God has placed upon us; worship gives us strength to present ourselves in this world as believers and thus, with our fellow believers, work out our salvation before God's face. Now, most Reformed people attend church faithfully and willingly. However, even among us, a subjectivistic element is not wholly absent. Many of us will flock to hear a particular preacher whose manner is in vogue and who is presently attracting and fascinating many people. It is possible, in this following, to neglect one's calling to participate in the service in one unified and integrated congregation, and so to neglect or deny the office of believer. A religious meeting with a good speaker is no substitute for the official, God-ordained worship service, which is a specific expression of the covenant and of office.

With one's baptism and confession in a given church, one is indeed saying that one's official place and calling are there. Unthinking attendance here, there, and everywhere undermines this reality. In no other area of life in which one has an office to fulfill is one so lax.

Another phenomenon related to church attendance also shows our insensitivity to office. This is the wide-spread pattern of church attendance only once on Sunday. One might argue that there are no clear-cut biblical injunctions concerning church attendance.

But this argument misses the point. The Bible does not give ready-made answers to all specific questions. If one allows Scripture to speak, one hears the constant admonition to be diligent in the service of the Lord. And then one must ask whether true zeal for the Lord is being expressed in one's meager church attendance.

If the congregation gathers on the Lord's day in order to meet God in the service of worship as people of God, then this is a gathering by which believers fulfill their calling and manifest their spiritual unity in the service of God. Worship is the meeting together of the confessors of the Lord's name. If I am a member of the congregation, then *we* are meeting together. It is only right and fitting that I am there, and there in the fullest sense of the word, it is in this way that we know and manifest our unity.

Of course there are extenuating circumstances, such as illness, which prevent one from full attendance in the church. Mothers with small children may also be prevented from full participation in the church. We could go on to cite all kinds of matters that hinder attendance twice per Sunday, and admonish one another to be careful in our judgment. On the other hand, these things should not cause the assembling of the church to be neglected.

One's office of believer is and remains an office in the assembly, the assembly of the congregation of which one is and will remain a living member. There, the believer's voice speaks, and sings; his prayers are brought before God's throne; his ears hear the Word, and his heart responds to God in the preaching; his contributions are added to the offerings; and the blessing in the name of the Triune God is pronounced upon him.

God can grant a blessing apart from these things, of course. But He does not do so, for He does not act in conflict with His own ordained institution. When one is shirking one's office there is a breach in the fellowship. The congregation feels it, and God takes note of it. Is the assembling of the Lord with His people not special enough for us? The office of believer should elicit something better from us.

This includes children too. It is sometimes said that children cannot get much out of a service. There is some truth in this. Yet I wonder whether children derive more from the worship service than we expect them to.

Let us assume that a child's conscious participation in the worship service is minimal, limited to singing and maybe reciting the Apostles Creed. Even if he did little more than read in his pew-Bible, and sit quietly looking around, he could still report that he was in church with his parents and siblings and that the pastor had explained about the Lord Jesus.

How highly should we value this experience? Certainly as highly as the "Hosanna to the Son of David" sung by the children in Jerusalem who were imitating their parents. They did not know consciously what they were doing. And yet Jesus said that God was preparing praise for Himself from the mouths of these children.

The concept of office gives the last word on this: These children stand in the office of believers and even now do so in the congregation. They have been incorporated into the Church of Christ and separated from other peoples and religions. So when the congregation is assembled, they belong to it. Their presence is by itself valuable, apart from what they as individuals may perform or contribute. We might recall the story of what an old deaf pastor said when he was asked why he should still attend church every Sunday when he couldn't hear a thing. He said, "The Lord loves to see me there." We can say, likewise, that the Lord loves to see His little children there.

Participation in Worship

In some circles, the administrative functions of the special offices so strongly dominate the church that believers are passive. They come only to listen, and to present an offering. The congregation seems to believe that the church is a project of the special office, which we must support, since we do reap some benefits.

Sometimes leaders try to combat this kind of passivity providing for more active congregational involvement. But does it help that a member steps forward and reads the Law or the Confession of Faith or a portion of Scripture? The crucial question is whether such efforts are necessary to give expression to the office of believers in the service of worship. I doubt it very much. The office of believers expresses itself in the worship service in wholly other ways, especially in those ways in which the Reformed service differs from the Roman Catholic service. In the latter, the office of believer is wholly depreciated. In the Catholic service, the celebrant *is* the church. The people are the objects of his priestly office; the receivers, while he is the giver. The leading idea is that in and through the sacraments the priest imparts grace to the people. Functioning as recepticals, they contribute nothing except their money and their devoted attention.

Over against this situation, the Reformers insisted on the centrality of the Word instead of the sacraments. The Reformers also recovered the meaning of the worship service as the meeting of God with His people. The gifts of the congregation were no longer regarded as a payment for the work of the priest but became a bringing of offerings to the Lord for His service and for the poor. Perhaps most important, congregational singing became an integral part of the worship service, providing for an active expression of praise and worship.

Furthermore, the Reformed congregation participates actively in its celebration of the Lord's Supper as a deed of faith and in its bringing of children to the congregation for baptism, a pledge of their faithfulness in response to the sealing of the covenant.

Together, the congregation prays. Certainly the minister of the Word speaks the prayer, but he speaks on behalf of the congregation and the congregation is thus active in this through the mouthpiece of the pastor. For many people, their participation becomes more meaningful when several persons besides the pastor lead in prayer or in the confession of faith. However, this does not make an essential difference. The congregation participates as actively in the execution of the office when the preacher performs these functions.

In the Reformed worship service, the main emphasis falls on the preaching of the Word. This does not minimize the sacraments; we acknowledge that the sacraments seal the Word even as it is continually proclaimed. Does hearing the Word mean passivity? By no means. Of course, if the congregation simply allows the preaching to pour over it like a torrent or stream of words, then indeed they are not exercising the office of believer. The proper administration of the Word is only well observed when the congregation understands that the Lord is coming to His people in His Word and that they have come to God to hear the message, to assimilate it and to take it to heart.

Hearing God's Word is not only an activity of the first order but the only activity befitting humans in relationship to their God. A relation of equality never exists between God and His people; however that fact in no way detracts from the dignity or office of the believer. Therefore, when in the administration of the Word, this relationship between speaking God and listening man shines forth, then the office of believer is most beautifully displayed and exercised.

Thus we are not called to find a liturgy in which preaching is minimized so that the congregation can be given a more obvious role. The congregation's duty is to listen. Rather, we are to practice improving and increasing our ability to listen, so that the congregation may listen to the Word with all its heart and soul and mind. That is not a slight task.

God always speaks to the congregation in human words. Embedded in human life, revelation speaks to us. At the center of sacred biblical history are the life and words of Jesus Himself. We also have the apostolic letters and the prophets, in which the Lord speaks directly to us in many ways. And we have divine revelation given to us in other forms that require biblical knowledge, discernment, reflection, and experience so that we may understand God's Word to us in our own times.

Thus, the reading and searching of Scripture requires of us much active, persistent exercise of our office as believers. In much the same way, hearing the preacher also requires an active exercise of the office of believer, for the preacher speaks, albeit imperfectly, as God's mouthpiece.

Actively exercising his office, the believer shall in the preached Word hear and discern the Word of God, distinguishing between it and the garb in which the human speaker transmits it. Sometimes this can be difficult. But when someone objects that the congregation never attains to the Word of God through the words of the preacher, we must insist on what Scripture itself says and what God promises to those who proclaim and hear and believe His Word. The congregation does indeed hear the Word of God, even though it is true sometimes that the speaker's words remain suspended in midair. Certainly the preacher must be wise and careful in his proclamation.

Because this saving reality exists, even under imperfect preaching, an expectant congregation can experience rich blessing, provided that the Word of God has been spoken. But whoever hears empty sounds because his heart is not receptive to the preaching of the Word is neglecting his office and is responsible for his own and others' spiritual detriment. Conversely, in the listening of the assembled congregation each believer is actively working for the good of the worship service and is therefore far from passive.

But the office of believer does not become visible only in cooperation in the worship service. It also functions in the total life of the church. First, there is the on-going reformation of the church. The very name of the reformed churches emphasizes continual progress and cooperation toward constructive change. It is customary in the yearbooks of our churches to list the names of those who founded each church congregation with the statement: these brethren separated themselves from the official church of the land. Their action was taken by virtue of the office of believer. In the tradition of Kuyper and Rutgers we believe that though the church is lead by the special office, believers do not have to subject themselves blindly to that office.

On the contrary, it can happen that the special office embodied in the consistory forsakes the right way and yields to error, even while intending to serve the truth. This was the situation in the official Reformed Church of The Netherlands in the days before the *Doleantie* and *Afscheiding*.

Kuyper, especially, believed that one does not as an individual member of the church separate oneself from its decay, but that one must bring the church back to reformation. One must make an attempt to persuade the whole of its error and bring it back to confession and a well ordered ecclesiastical life. If at all possible the reforming brethren would move the consistory to suspend obedience to the higher authorities, while continuing to act as consistory of the local congregation. In this way, members might follow these faithful office-bearers and with them work to bring the congregation back to the path of truth.

If the whole consistory could not be so moved, then efforts were made to bring part of the consistory, with the congregation, to repentance and renewed consciousness. Sometimes, of course, not one of the office-bearers felt the urgency to yield. Then sometimes individual members would assert themselves as leaders of the reform and invite their fellow believers to return to the correct form of ecclesiastical life.

To establish that this was not in conflict with the obedience that is owing to the special office, those who chose this route appealed to the fact that everyone in the congregation bore office; thus they could speak of a renewal or reformation by virtue of the office of all believers. By virtue of this reformational principle, these persons rejected the difference between clergy and laity. With respect for the special dignity of the three offices instituted by Christ and His apostles, they nevertheless maintained the principle of the general priesthood of all believers.